TEACHING THE TEACHERS

TEACHING THE TEACHERS

A DIY Training Course for those
involved in children's ministry

SUSAN SAYERS

kevin
mayhew

First published in 2002 by
KEVIN MAYHEW LTD
Buxhall, Stowmarket, Suffolk IP14 3BW
Email: info@kevinmayhewltd.com

© 2002 Susan Sayers

The right of Susan Sayers to be identified as the author
of this work has been asserted by her in accordance
with the Copyright, Designs and Patents Act 1988.

All rights reserved. No part of this publication may be
reproduced, stored in a retrieval system, or transmitted,
in any form or by any means, electronic, mechanical,
photocopying, recording or otherwise, without the prior
written permission of the publisher.

The Scripture quotations contained herein are from the
New Revised Standard Version Bible, copyright © 1989,
by the Division of Christian Education of the National Council
of the Churches of Christ in the USA, and are used by permission.
All rights reserved.

9 8 7 6 5 4 3 2 1 0

ISBN 1 84003 970 1
Catalogue No 1500541

Cover design by Angela Selfe
Edited by Katherine Laidler
Typesetting by Louise Selfe
Printed and bound in Great Britain

Contents

Introduction	7
Daily prayer outline	9
Preparation reading for session 1	11
Session 1: *What are we trying to do?*	16
Preparation reading for session 2	25
Session 2: *What's the best way to go about it?*	30
Preparation reading for session 3	39
Session 3: *Growing together in faith*	45
Preparation reading for session 4	51
Session 4: *Ways of telling the story*	56
Preparation reading for session 5	64
Session 5: *Behaviour management*	71
Preparation reading for session 6	77
Session 6: *When we're all together*	83
Review and refresh	90
Appendix: Useful resources	93

Introduction

We all recognise how important it is to include children and young people in our churches. We want them to be part of the worship, teaching and faith nurture of the whole community. But for many of us this causes a problem. Perhaps only a very few children and young people come to our church at the moment. Perhaps the adults in the church don't feel up to the task of changing that. 'What are we to do?' I often hear. 'I'm no longer young, and no one else is volunteering to take it on. They're frightened of being stuck with it for ever, like I was!'

The tiredness, frustration and longing for something better is often desperate and it is widespread.

With shifting patterns of life, either people work right up to their margins already and have no extra space and time to commit, or the effect of long-term unemployment and economic hardship undermines people's confidence. Something else I hear a lot is this: 'I don't mind helping out sometimes but I certainly wouldn't be able to lead or take charge.' Even with those persuaded to take on the responsibility or share the workload, training courses may be some distance away and difficult to get to on a regular basis. And how can churches be expected to provide their own training for these helpers?

These are real fears and real problems, and no amount of wishing will make them go away.

During many years of training days around the country I have been greatly impressed with the way so many small church communities refuse to give in to the difficulties. They work faithfully and creatively, often in incredibly basic conditions, in order to include children and young people week by week. Picking up on all kinds of good practice I have discovered in rural and urban communities, I have tried to provide here the sort of support and help which seems to be most needed. This DIY training course is simple to use and very flexible:

- It enables a church to start where it is already, rather than wishing it was somewhere else.
- All participants learn together so there is no need for anyone to be an expert.
- The sessions can be fitted in to a schedule which matches the lives of those taking part, so that everyone can complete all the course at their own pace.
- The main course is only six sessions long, so any new helpers and leaders can work through it before they join an existing team.
- **Each participant has their own copy of this book** which builds into a personal handbook to help them in their subsequent ministry.
- Suggestions are provided for follow-up study and practice, discussion and regular review.
- The emphasis is on faith nurture in the whole church community, so the course enables people to deepen their own faith at the same time as preparing them for helping children and young people.
- Even those not directly involved with children and young people can join in the learning so that the commitment is owned by the whole church community.

Susan Sayers

Daily prayer outline

Use this prayer guide each day.
If you learn it by heart you can do it anywhere.

> Before you start talking with God,
> quieten your thinking and planning,
> and remember that God's love is all around you
> and in every crevice of the universe.

Say the Lord's Prayer SLOWLY, thinking about what you are saying.
Say it in any form, and preferably in your mother tongue.

Our Father in heaven . . .
hallowed be your name . . .
your kingdom come . . .
your will be done on earth as in heaven . . .
Give us today our daily bread . . .
and forgive us our sins
as we forgive those who sin against us . . .
Lead us not into temptation
but set us free from evil . . .
For the kingdom, the power and the glory
are yours for ever and ever.
Amen.

Now praise God and thank him for all that is good and faithful, just and true. Do this in your own words or these.

Glory to the Father
and to the Son
and to the Holy Spirit!
As it was in the beginning,
is now . . .
and shall be for ever.
Amen.

Now pray for people and situations in need of God's healing and transforming love.
Pray by name for the others on this course.
Pray for the children and young people at your church.

The Lord is my shepherd; there is nothing else I need. (Psalm 23)
Blessed be God for ever!
Amen.

Preparation reading for session 1

If anyone has a reading difficulty, please pair them up with a reading partner.

> Welcome to this DIY Co-op Training Course for those involved, directly or indirectly, with children and young people in the church community.
>
> This course is designed so you do not need an 'expert' or a 'leader'. Instead, all of you learn from one another co-operatively, using the material provided. Additionally, you each bring to the course your own life and faith experience so far, whatever that may be, and your ongoing prayers for the children and young people in your area and their families, and for the church. This means that there will be different ground rules in this course from one in which you are led from the front. Let's start with prayer . . .

Heavenly Father,
   you already know and love
   each person in this community.
We ask that through our church
   the whole community may be blessed.
We pray especially for the babies, the toddlers,
   the children and the young people,
   and those who care for them.
May they all come to know
   how much you love them.
May they get to know you so well

> that the friendship lasts throughout their lives
> and on into heaven.
> Amen.

1. Use the course to suit your own needs

We all own this course and so can use it to scratch where we itch, rather than having an imposed and controlled format. Accordingly, it is quite acceptable to spend longer on some sessions than others, and follow up some leads in more detail, while touching more lightly on others. In any case, there are slots throughout each session for you and your group to do the thinking and talking, and these are not an added extra but an important part of the training. In a sense each group is writing its own course as it goes along, enabled by the material provided. It is more like a self-drive with vouchers than a package holiday.

2. The co-op habit

The course aims to get you working together and supporting each other co-operatively during the sessions so that you get into the co-op habit, ready for a healthy, sustainable ministry when the course has finished. This means that the importance of practicalities like organisation and hospitality are taken seriously and need to be shared fairly, rather than one person being left with too heavy a workload. At the first session there are checklists provided for all these jobs, and you'll find that co-operative good practice will become second nature by the working methods you use throughout the training as well as by what you are taught.

3. The talking stick

In many ancient tribal traditions elders have a talking stick in all their community meetings. Only the one holding the stick may talk; the task of the rest is to listen! The stick is passed around the group so that all contributions are included without the pressure of getting your word in before someone else speaks, or over-dominance by any one speaker. In a co-op course like this, all members share the responsibility for ensuring that everyone is heard, and no one dominates. This is such a valuable skill to learn for healthy, sustainable ministry, and one in short supply in our culture! Throughout the course you will be reminded of it, so that another good habit is in place to be continued in all your other life areas.

4. Different but still valid

We will not find we agree with one another about everything! We all come from different backgrounds and experience, and our personalities are wonderfully varied, just as much as what we look like. This is something to celebrate. But Christians are notorious for trying to pretend conflict doesn't and shouldn't exist, and they often feel guilty when it happens. During this course the issue of conflict is addressed, and throughout all sessions we can practise good ways of disagreeing lovingly with one another, respecting differences and acknowledging that other ways of thinking and doing may be different from ours, but may well be still equally valid.

5. Body parts

This training course takes place in the context of our whole church community. We may be the ones directly involved with the children and young people, but the whole church needs to be involved in its attitude to and understanding of the different age groups. And the whole church shares the responsibility of prayer. Once again, the course aims to cultivate lasting habits of good practice, so throughout the training each of you needs to find a prayer supporter willing to be committed to praying for you and your family during the time the sessions are running. Others in the church will pray for the local area, for the children and young people and their families. There are résumés of each session to print on news sheets so everyone is informed and feels part of what is going on.

6. Growing in faith

You will not find this course to be a potted teacher training manual adapted for churches. That is because I think we have too long equated any ministry involving children and young people with a school model. Even in these 'post-Sunday School' days the expectation of 'mature adults passing on the faith to the immature young' still lingers. In my experience the reality is that often adults whose faith is just beginning to grow again – perhaps after many years of neglect – are the ones now getting involved, and our young people, as ever, are excited by the deep questions and are sensitive to the spiritual. If the church really is a community of Christ's love in which we all help each other to grow in faith, then a training course needs to reflect this in its co-operative nature, and in the recognition that such ministry is a shared journey, where our own commitment to spiritual growth is essential. So this course addresses our own deepening faith, with the understanding that the homework which goes on between sessions includes guided prayer, Bible study and reflection.

7. Children are welcome

For some of you the training sessions can be arranged while your children are at nursery, playgroup or school. For others the babies and children will come along as well. I don't see a problem in this. We just need to make sure that we are providing for the needs of everyone there, whatever the age. It helps to have a couple of extra adults sitting in on the sessions to be available for playing and so on, and I have written into each session suggestions for ways to involve the children from time to time. It's important that the children enjoy coming.

8. What you will need for session 1

Each person needs:
- their own copy of the course book
- a Bible
- a photograph of themselves as a child and photographs of any children at this session

The group needs:
- large sheets of paper (flipchart pages or some lining paper)

- felt-tip pens/crayons
- pens/pencils

Optional extras:
- CD/tape player and music to play for worship

Checklist for session 1

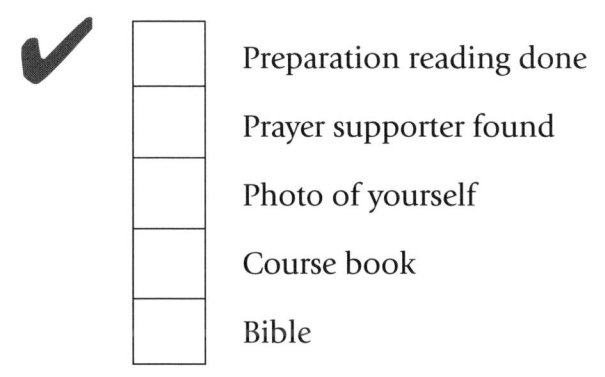

☐ Preparation reading done

☐ Prayer supporter found

☐ Photo of yourself

☐ Course book

☐ Bible

This week's Bible reading: Matthew 18:1-5

At that time the disciples came to Jesus and asked, 'Who is the greatest in the kingdom of heaven?' He called a child, whom he put among them, and said, 'Truly I tell you, unless you change and become like children, you will never enter the kingdom of heaven. Whoever becomes humble like this child is the greatest in the kingdom of heaven. Whoever welcomes one such child in my name welcomes me.'

To think over . . .

Children had no status and no power in the society Jesus was addressing. Kingdoms traditionally have a group of powerful henchmen around the king. Imagine the passage above as if you were watching it taking place. What do you think Jesus is saying about the kingdom of heaven, and what is he wanting to get straight with his band of disciples?

Session 1
What are we trying to do?

Learning outcomes

By the end of this session we will have
- introduced ourselves
- prayed together
- organised practicalities
- explored what this ministry is all about
- agreed on our aim as children's and young people's leaders in the church
- celebrated what we have and recognised what we need

Introductions (10 minutes)

If your children are with you, set up in the room places for drawing and colouring, building and so on, but let them stay with you until they feel ready to move off to play.

Place everyone's photos on a table and enjoy guessing who they belong to. Include the children if they wish.

If the group is small, introduce yourselves, sharing perhaps something which really saddens you and something which makes you laugh. With larger groups split into smaller groups for this.

Prayer (5 minutes)

Play some quiet worship music on CD or tape to give everyone a chance to settle into God's company. Now follow together the daily prayer outline on page 9, with this week's reading.

SESSION 1: WHAT ARE WE TRYING TO DO?

Practical organisation (5 minutes)

Over the course there are various things to be done and provided, and these need to be shared out right away.

Responsibility for:	Session 1	Session 2	Session 3	Session 4	Session 5	Session 6
Home to meet in						
Refreshments						
Leading the worship						
Leading the session						
Time keeper						
Help with children						

What is this ministry all about? (70 minutes including refreshments)

Reader

Even if we have been involved with children's work for many years, it's useful sometimes to step aside and ask ourselves this question. The thinking we go through and the answers we come up with will help us with all our work and planning, and make sure it really is in keeping with what we feel is most important, rather than just doing what has always been done, or what we have been bequeathed by the last people who did it.

Let's start with the very basic, and most important question of all.

> What have you discovered about God?
> What do you think God is like?

Group action

Write the words 'GOD IS . . .' in the middle of a large sheet of paper. Now share your thoughts about the question and write everyone's thoughts around these words, using different colours. (Children can join in, drawing their ideas.)

Copy what is written on the sheet into your own course book, thinking about the words as you write them. You might like to play some music while you do this without speaking. God is making himself known to you as a group.

GOD IS . . .

Reader

In the light of what we have shared together about our own faith in God, let's look next at what we want and long for where our children and young people are concerned – as people with the whole of the rest of their lives to live. (Don't drift into Sunday morning stuff yet – stay with the bigger issue at the moment, please.)

Group action

Think about the children at your church, and those who don't come, and the world they are growing up in. What is your hope and prayer for them in their lives now and in the future? Jot down the thoughts of everyone – in note form – so that everyone has them in their own book.

> We hope and pray that . . .

Reader

Sometimes it's tempting to jump straight into the practical 'doing' before we've thought out what we're aiming at. But that's a bit like enthusiastically packing a suitcase and then finding it's too heavy to lift, and the things you want to use first are right at the bottom. It's good sense to be really clear about our aims before we start a job. That way we can choose the best methods and materials and avoid expensive mistakes.

Now that we have reminded ourselves of the God we know and love, and seen what we really want for our children, we can begin to establish what we are trying to do in our ministry with children in church.

So we are going to focus our aim in a sentence. This can then be used as a kind of ruler, to measure up everything we do involving children and young people in our church, so it's worth making sure it really reflects what we feel is important.

- Use the hopes and prayers which came up in your discussion
- Keep in mind your particular church and its tradition
- Keep in mind the area your church is in

Group action

While you have some refreshments, work together on a statement which sums up what you now feel your ministry with children and young people is all about.

OUR AIM . . .

SESSION 1: WHAT ARE WE TRYING TO DO?

Reader

In the light of your agreed aim, have a look at the following models of ministry involving children and young people on a Sunday morning.

St Agatha's

> The children have their own separate service in the church hall and join the rest of the congregation for refreshments afterwards. The young people from the whole area have their separate worship together, supported by the different churches. They meet their congregations on a few special occasions a year.

St Mungo's

> The children and young people are in church with their families the whole time, and we include them in everything. There is a crèche area in church for the very young children.

St Wilbert's

> The children and young people have their own teaching during the readings and sermon, but are included in all the rest of the service. Sometimes they pray in their own age groups during the prayers.

St Ursula's

> The children and young people meet in the hall 10 minutes before the service for their own teaching and worship, based on the day's readings. They come into church at the sharing of the Peace and are then included in the rest of the worship, bringing any art/craft/drama/music.

St Boniface's

> The children are in the service for a hymn and short talk before leaving to learn and worship on their own. The young people help them. They come in again at the end to show what they have been doing. They may sing a song or show their art/craft. Everyone claps them.

St Magnus's

> We encourage the children and young people to serve, sing in the choir, read and lead prayers like everyone else. We give them a handout to help them with the readings at their level, but want them to catch the atmosphere of worship. Their clubs are during the week.

Things to bear in mind . . .

1. What signals are the children and young people getting about their place and role in the church?
2. Worship or performance?
3. Is anyone not being nurtured in faith here?

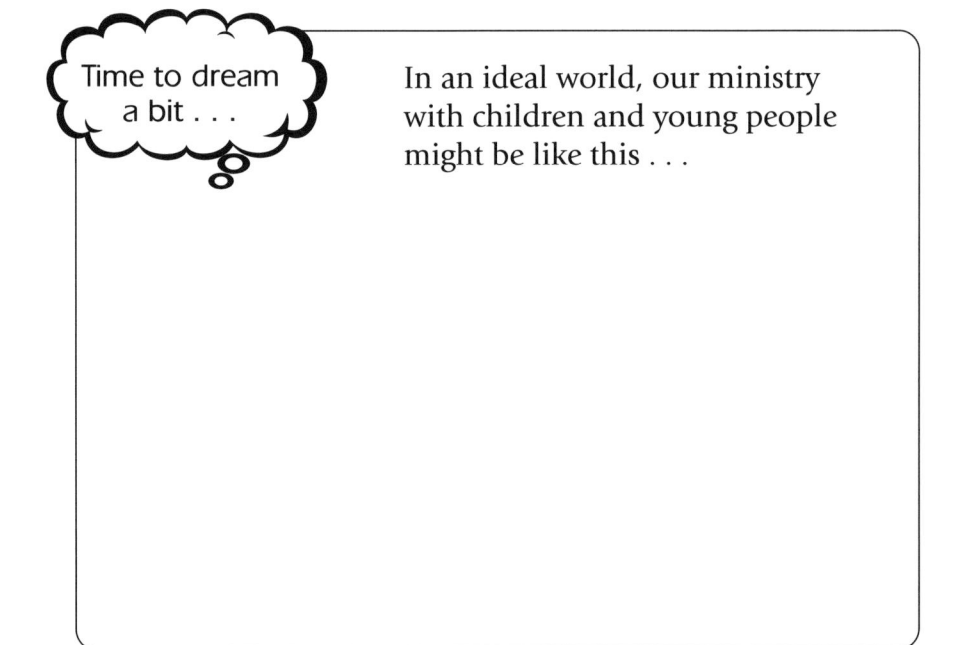

Time to dream a bit . . .

In an ideal world, our ministry with children and young people might be like this . . .

> Time to celebrate a bit . . .
>
> Count your bread and fishes – in other words, instead of looking at all the problems, make a list of all the things you *can* offer the children and young people at your church.

To finish

Read Matthew 14:13-21

This is the word of the Lord.

**Thanks be to God
who accepts what we can offer
and uses it for the feeding of many.
Amen.**

Group action

- Arrange for one person to give a copy of the agreed aim to the priest or minister and a copy of the summary to the editor of the weekly news sheet.
- Arrange for someone to stick a copy of the aim on the inside door of your resources cupboard.
- Ensure that everyone has an appropriate Disclosure form to complete before the next session, and a copy of the church's Child Protection Policy to read.
- Remind each other of the date and place of the next session, and whose responsibility it will be to provide refreshments and so on.

Summary for the weekly news sheet

> **The DIY Co-op Training Course**
>
> At our first session we thought about our aims, and the reasons why we believe this work is important. We've come up with this statement: (Insert your agreed aim)
>
> Session 2 will be on (date) at (time), meeting at (address). Please keep us all in your prayers. Thank you.

Preparation reading for session 2

If anyone has a reading difficulty, please pair them up with a reading partner

Heavenly Father,
   you already know and love
   each person in this community.
We ask that through our church
   the whole community may be blessed.
We pray especially for the babies, the toddlers,
   the children and the young people,
   and those who care for them.
May they all come to know
   how much you love them.
May they get to know you so well
   that the friendship lasts throughout their lives
   and on into heaven.
Amen.

1. What kind of person are you?

We're all different in the way we do things and in how we think. Some of us like to plan everything in advance and weigh up the different options carefully before making any choices. Others of us prefer to go more by what feels right, and keep all options flexible so that we're free to react to any unforeseen events. Some like to know exactly what's happening, and others like an element of surprise. Some of us notice every detail, and others of us are good at seeing the overall picture. For some it's very important that *Things Are Done Properly*, while for others what matters most is that everyone feels loved and included, even if that means expecting a few mistakes or notes being sung out of tune.

You've probably noticed that although you've learned to work in your less preferred way sometimes, that can feel more like hard work for you, whereas working in the way you naturally feel comfortable seems to give you more energy and fulfilment.

As our own methods of living are very familiar to us – we've lived with them all our life, after all – we often assume that our way of doing things is really the only right way, and those who do things differently haven't quite got themselves sorted out. We might even feel it's our duty to help the others work as we do – the 'best' way.

But, of course, the truth is that God made us all different and there are pluses and minuses for all the different ways. Usually a community works best when all these differences work together for the good of all. And doesn't that sound a bit like what Paul wrote in one of his letters to the Christians in Corinth? 'Now there are varieties of gifts, but the same Spirit; and there are varieties of services, but the same Lord; and there are varieties of activities, but it is the same God who activates all of them in everyone' (1 Corinthians 12:4-6). In fact, Paul goes on to say that the really 'best' way is actually the way of love – and love involves respecting one another, and learning to live together in God's harmony.

2. How can we best work together?

It's a good idea to make ourselves more aware of the different ways we work, and recognise what one another's gifts are. So spend a bit of time this week noticing the way you run your life, which things drain you quickly and which you look forward to and find satisfying. Notice the methods of working that irritate you and see if they are anything to do with a simple personality difference. (If so, try thinking of them more as 'different' than 'wrong', which may help you respect their alternative way of going about things, and will also lower your stress levels!)

Be positive – think of the things you value and admire about the other members of the group, jotting these down if this helps you. Practise living by this way of love which Jesus showed us, being ready to notice the good in people, and using any irritations as good practice opportunities for forgiveness and self-knowledge.

The other thing about working well together is recognising that part of living in love is working through the unavoidable difficulties and conflicts, rather than pretending there aren't any. That's far more healthy, and far more creative as well.

During the next session we will be looking at how you can best organise the work God has given you, using everyone's natural strengths and gifts.

3. Using that aim

Have a look over your notes from the last session, and as you use the daily prayer guide during the week, lay the written aim out in front of you, so that you bring it quite literally 'before God in prayer'. You're going to use this aim a bit like a measuring stick. Anything which looks as if it might help further your aim – try it out. Anything which goes completely against your aim – chuck it out!

4. Praying for one another

As you pray for people regularly there's a by-product. It's increased love. I don't really understand how this happens, but I'm not a bit surprised about it. God's love seems to spill out and get absorbed into any situation we pray about, so that we often become part of the answer. So whenever we pray for a person we gradually find ourselves understanding and loving them more, and, if there have been difficulties in the relationship, that deepening love is a great healer of wounds. This is not usually a speedy process but a cumulative one, so rather than immediate results it's more like the smooth, rounded pebbles worked on by the daily tides and shingle. But that's God again, isn't it – both love and faithfulness together!

We need to pray for our co-workers in ministry, and we also need them to pray for us. Being prayed for faithfully and daily is like an ongoing gift – like being given a year's subscription as a Christmas present so we can go on enjoying it all through the year. Set up this habit of prayer for one another during the course, so that it goes on and on afterwards. Include not only those you work well with but also those with whom the sparks fly; any in the church you feel resent the children and young people; any who seem to put obstacles in the way; any who engage in power games. (And, yes, all this does happen in other church communities as well as yours! We are not a perfect community of love, but a community of love with L plates.) Don't forget to keep in contact with your prayer partner, and include plenty of thanksgiving in your prayer as well as the requests.

5. What you will need for session 2

Each person needs:
- their own copy of the course book
- a Bible

The group needs:
- playdough and Lego bricks
- appropriate Disclosure forms, completed, and copies of the Child Protection Policy
- large sheets of paper (flipchart pages or some lining paper)
- felt-tip pens/crayons
- pens/pencils

Optional extras:
- CD/tape player and music to play for worship

Checklist for session 2

✔
☐	Preparation reading done
☐	Prayer supporter contacted
☐	Playdough and Lego organised
☐	Completed Disclosure forms
☐	Course book

PREPARATION READING FOR SESSION 2

☐ Bible

☐ Daily prayer

This week's Bible reading: Mark 10:42-45

So Jesus called them and said to them, 'You know that among the Gentiles those whom they recognise as their rulers lord it over them, and their great ones are tyrants over them. But it is not so among you; but whoever wishes to become great among you must be your servant, and whoever wishes to be the first among you must be slave of all. For the Son of Man came not to be served but to serve, and to give his life a ransom for many.'

To think over . . .

What has this to say about the way we organise things in our churches?

Session 2
What's the best way to go about it?

Learning outcomes

By the end of this session we will have
- prayed and played together
- recognised the structures and boundaries we are working within
- looked at appropriate and effective organisation of time, space and resources
- recognised our own need of support and realistic planning
- looked at whole church involvement

Introduction (10 minutes)

(If your children are with you, set up in the room places for drawing and colouring, building and so on, but let them stay with you until they feel ready to move off to play. They can join in the first activity with the adults.)

You will need some playdough and some Lego.

1. Roll some playdough into long thin worms and try making this shape with them:

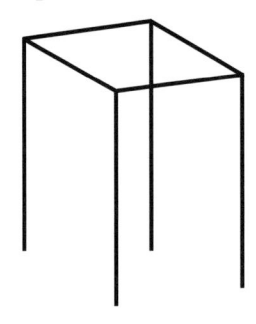

2. Try joining Lego bricks together to make the shape of a circle.
3. Give an extra biscuit to the best ones!

Reader

OK, so that was just silly. We were given a nearly impossible task! But actually working with the materials means you can physically feel the problem: too much organisational structure makes it difficult or impossible to respond to changing needs, and too little leads to a rather formless sloppiness that sags; things may go right, but they may go disastrously wrong.

Prayer (5 minutes)

Play some quiet worship music on CD or tape to give everyone a chance to settle into God's company.

Now follow together the daily prayer outline on page 9.

Practical organisation (up to 5 minutes)

Check that the Disclosure forms have been completed and returned to the nominated person in your church. Deal with any changes to dates, refreshments or other practical matters that have been made.

Organisation and planning that works effectively (70 minutes including refreshments)

Reader

This is a question of putting in place organisation of time, space, money and help that is *appropriate*. It needs to be firm enough for everyone to be safe, to feel they know where they are and what is expected of them. It needs to be flexible and sustainable, with as little 'red tape' as possible. That goes for all the children and young people, and for all the adults involved. Effective organisation frees us up from the stressful panic just before an event, and from unnecessarily anxious moments when more children turn up than we expected, someone is unexpectedly unable to be there on time, or we can't find the first aid box or a home phone number when we need it fast. It means that in the event of an emergency we can follow a procedure agreed during a time of calm, and we don't need to feel we are lurching from crisis to crisis.

We'll now look at the different areas of appropriate organisation and planning.

1. Safety

Safety is the basic requirement: organising an environment in which everyone is safe. Since we are followers of the God of truth and justice, faithfulness and love, it goes without saying that the church needs to be utterly scrupulous about this. Every baby, child, young person and adult, should find churches to be communities in which trust develops and is never abused. Every leader and helper, and the whole church, needs to be aware of the Child Protection Policy and the nominated person. Everyone involved with children and young people in the church, both paid and voluntary, needs to have completed and returned the appropriate Disclosure form.

The nominated person in our church is:

_____

☐   I have read the Child Protection Policy for our church

Group action

What structures must be organised to ensure (as far as possible) everyone's safety?

You might like to discuss this in different sections:

┌───┐
│   The building and grounds   │
│   │
│   │
└───┘

> Adequate supervision

> Child protection

> Activities

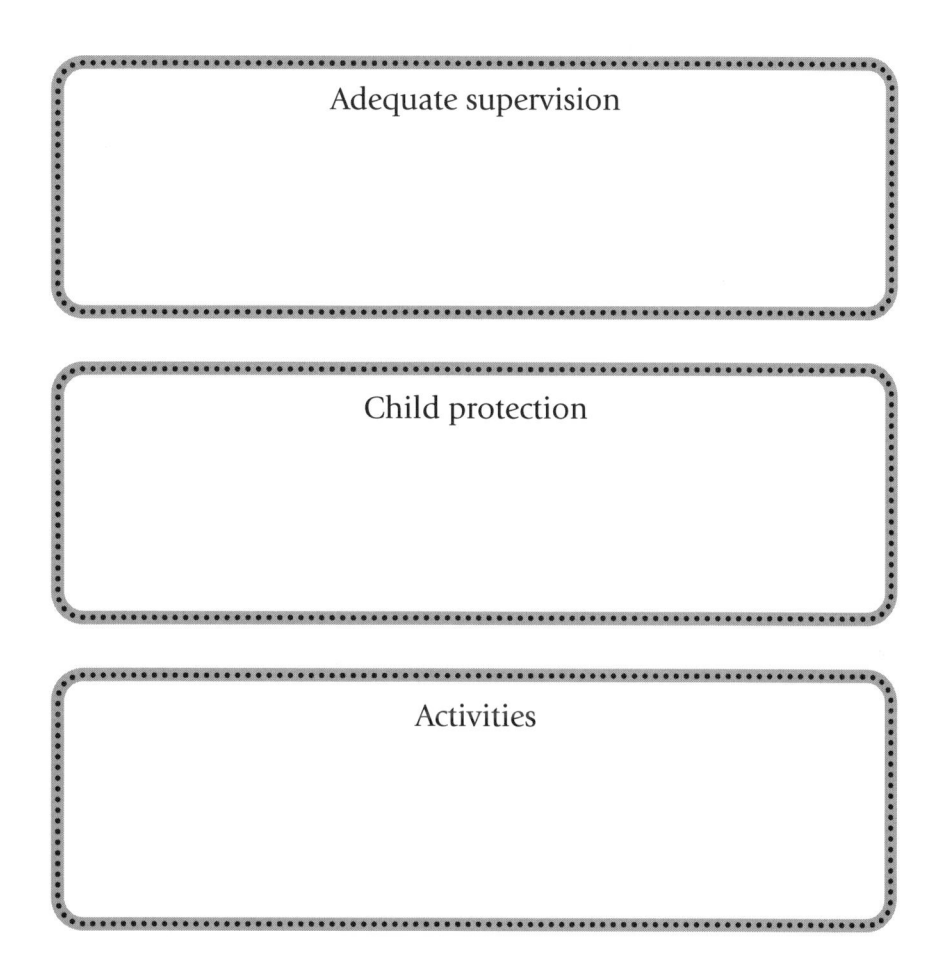

Reader

It must also be said that we need to be protected from over-protective policies. Right and necessary as it is to safeguard and protect our young from danger, it would be damaging to children if, for instance, all touch were to be considered wrong within a community of trust, and if all sense of adventure and challenge were excluded. We need to be sensible about this and avoid throwing the baby out with the bath water.

2. Planning the use of time, space and resources

So that your time with the children can be as valuable as possible, it is sensible to plan

    a) who does what, when, where and how

    b) use of resources

and write your decisions down in some kind of information sheet or policy document, under your aim. Copies need to be given to everyone – in a folder or wallet – so they can all refer to it and everyone knows what has been agreed. That way there are fewer misunderstandings, and we don't have to overtax our memories either. It's also important that the rest of the congregation are invited to look at this, so that the whole church shares in this ministry.

Talk over together:

a) What structures are in place in our church which we cannot change and have to work with?

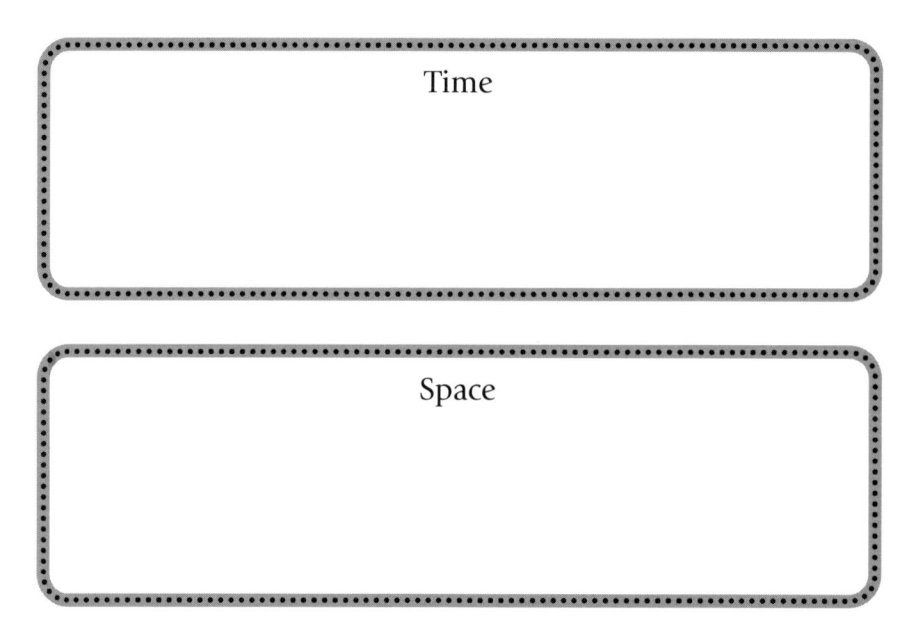

```
Time
```

```
Space
```

b) Within these boundaries we can organise ourselves how we want

i) Effective organisation of time

The challenges:

Often there is a lot to pack in to a short space of time. The amount of time we have may vary from week to week, according to who is preaching and so on. We want to avoid rushing through a programme, but we still want to provide the children and young people with authentic activities and teaching as part of the worship. Sound familiar?

Look at these suggested ways of dealing with the challenges:
- **Careful planning of each session** (Everyone knows exactly what they are doing and how long they have.)

- **Thorough preparation** (After the planning prepare your materials well in advance so that on Sunday morning you have only to pick them up and bring them.)
- **Enough for everyone** (Always over-estimate numbers and prepare enough, even if some don't get used that day.)
- **Completing a model is more satisfying than starting it** (If you know there isn't enough time to do a whole art/craft activity, prepare the first few stages in advance, so that the children can do the assembling, and get the satisfaction of completing it.)
- **Have a time-keeper** (Within each part of the programme as well as for the finish time, and give a warning a minute or two before it's time to clear up.)
- **Be realistic** (about what you can actually achieve in the time allowed – better to attempt less than try cramming in too much.)
- **Be flexible** (so that as a team you might agree to extend an activity which seems to be particularly valuable, and cut another part of the programme.)

. . . and add in your own ideas

ii) Effective organisation of space
The challenges:
I am constantly amazed by the creative use of appalling spaces made by those working with children and young people in churches! The space provided may be too far from the church, too small, too vast, inappropriately shared, heated or furnished.

Look at these suggested ways of dealing with the challenges:
- **Make a tour together of the space and look at it afresh** (Are there any areas which you could make better use of? Is some potential space filled with clutter that could be cleared? Would some new/different furnishings make all the difference, such as a carpet, worship area, plastic floor covering, chairs and tables?)

- **Make a list of what you would really like in your space** (Even if the wish-list seems impossible, it's worth talking to church leaders about these needs. There may be ways and means . . .)
- **Use different space areas in your programme** (Have a quiet and beautiful prayer area. Have age group or story areas clearly marked out on the floor. Use the walls as attractive display areas. Move the group from one space to another as part of the story telling sometimes.)

. . . and add in your own ideas

c) Effective organisation of resources
The challenge:
There is cost involved, in money, time and energy, and the whole church needs to own the ministry and this cost.

Look at these suggested ways of dealing with the challenge:
- **You will need a budget** (agreed at the church council so that you can plan the buying of equipment and ensure that all weekly running costs – such as copying – are paid by the church). This is urgent!
- **You will need lockable storage space** (A combination lock – with the number kept in a secret place – avoids problems of lost keys.)
- **Acquire basic stock** (There's a suggestion list with sources on page 93.)
- **Delegate and spread the workload** (It is never God's plan to have us collapsing from overwork and ending up leaving this ministry – or even church – because we're simply exhausted and worn down.)
- **Make a list of the kind of support you would really appreciate being in place** (and work together on setting this up).
- **Make this a whole church community ministry** (Encourage everyone to support you and the children and young people with their regular prayer, their welcome, and their response to

requests for yogurt pots or old shirts. Give regular feedback and invitations to see what's going on.)

. . . and add in your own ideas

3. Planning the planning

Careful and thorough weekly planning is clearly a must. It's always best to work together, as ideas bounce around and the session builds up your faith and your relationship with God and each other. In your planning meetings:

- arrange specific start and finish times and stick to them
- pray for the children and their families, the church, and each other
- read the Bible passages and share insights and questions
- share the tasks around and make a checklist of who is doing and bringing what

4. Recording your organisation in a policy document

Work through the following questions together, making notes of the answers you decide.

- What is our aim?
- How does this work fit into the general way our church welcomes children?
- When and where do we operate?
- Who is on the team? (names and contact numbers)
- What do they do if they can't make a date they are on duty? (back-ups, swaps?)
- What goes on? (Give details of the usual pattern)
- Who has responsibility for which jobs? (Register, birthday cards, locking up, contacting those absent)
- Which resource books do we use?
- Where are things kept?
- Where and when do we plan?

- What is our child safety policy and who is the nominated person?

This policy document should be reviewed and updated once a year.

To finish

Read Luke 19:29-35
This is the word of the Lord.
Thanks be to God
  who invites our help
  and involves us
  in his ordered provision.
Amen.

Group action

Arrange for one of you to make the notes up into a clear policy document, with copies (in plastic wallets) given to

- each of you
- the minister or priest
- the church council
- the parish magazine (copies of this to be given to all parents)

Summary for the weekly news sheet

The DIY Co-op Training Course
At our second session we came up with this policy document, based on our aim. Session 3 will be on (date) at (time), meeting at (address). Please keep us all in your prayers. Thank you.

Preparation reading for session 3

If anyone has a reading difficulty, please pair them up with a reading partner.

Heavenly Father,
   you already know and love
   each person in this community.
We ask that through our church
   the whole community may be blessed.
We pray especially for the babies, the toddlers,
   the children and the young people,
   and those who care for them.
May they all come to know
   how much you love them.
May they get to know you so well
   that the friendship lasts throughout their lives
   and on into heaven.
Amen.

1. What is faith?

Faith is not a body of knowledge. We can't burn the midnight oil studying to graduate in faith with honours. In fact, we could know a great deal about Jesus and have no faith in him at all. The gospels give us plenty of examples of people with great faith, little faith, and none, and often Jesus is found encouraging people in their faith ('Your faith has made you whole') and marvelling at how little faith his followers often have ('Oh you of little faith'; 'where is your faith?').

Christian faith is about an extraordinary relationship – the close, life-changing relationship we are able to have with the

One who made us and this habitat we call Universe. It's to do with our eyes being opened to notice and recognise the heavenly which is here all the time but often hidden. It's like putting on those glasses which allow us to see darkness as daylight. It's being able to live in the light and eternity of heaven even while we walk about here in our lives on earth.

And it all hinges on Jesus, who was a well-documented historical figure living 2000 years ago – a real person in a real, occupied country in the Middle East. During his life it became gradually clear that this man Jesus was not only a real human person; Jesus was also the Son of the one true God. He was the Messiah (or anointed one) who had been long expected by prophets, and he was God on earth announcing the reign of God on earth as well as in heaven. Living out God's love in the language of human behaviour which we find easier to understand, Jesus loved without compromise, so that he ended up dying the cursed death of Roman crucifixion. Three days later the unthinkable happened, and Jesus was seen by a large number of witnesses alive – but alive in a new way which we have not fully experienced yet. It is this new life which is offered us, through the Spirit of God.

2. We are all growing together

From the Sunday 'School' model of children and young people's ministry in churches, there is an underlying assumption that the adults, in their mature faith, are passing on 'the faith' to the children. In one way, of course, this is true. It is our duty and our joy to pass on to our children the faith we have discovered to be the source of full and abundant life. But in another sense it is misleading, as it assumes the adults are 'experts' and the children know nothing, and nothing could be further from the truth. It was, after all, a child Jesus used as an example of how we are to receive the kingdom of God. What really happens is that we are all growing in faith together throughout our lives, within the community of faith we know as the Church. We all need one another on this journey, and we travel as disciples, or students, with Jesus to teach and guide us on the way and as the Way.

During each lifetime there may be times when we are growing very little in faith – or think we are. In an odd way these may turn out to be the very times when we are growing most! Similarly the points when we begin to feel we are acquiring great spiritual maturity in faith may well turn out to be when we're not growing very much at all.

3. Your own faith journey

During this week think over your faith journey so far, and draw it as a line. It probably won't be a straight, steady line!

4. How do we grow in faith?

In the Bible and throughout the history of the Church we find examples of people who have suddenly 'seen the light' – like Paul on his way to Damascus, and John Wesley. Some have kicked against having faith for ages before believing almost in spite of themselves – like Augustine and C. S. Lewis. And some have grown from childhood into adulthood with a faith always lively, but simply in keeping with their physical and mental development – like Timothy and Mother Theresa. So it is clear that there are as many ways of growing in faith as there are people.

But there do seem to be patterns of growth, or development, which have been explored by such people as James Fowler and John Westerhoff, who have suggested various models to help us understand better what is going on. It's important to remember that they are only models, and although they help us in our thinking, they are by no means an exact description of what is going on.

James Fowler's Faith Stages

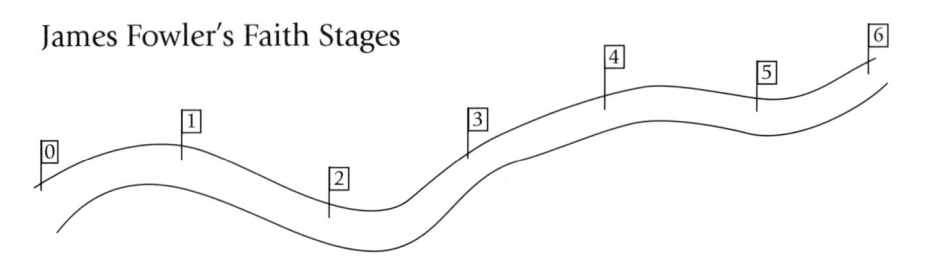

James Fowler sees this as sequential – a natural process of development, linked with cognitive and emotional development until the radical leap, through grace, made in stage 6 by only a few. These are the stages:

Stage 0: Primal faith

Stage 1: Intuitive – Projective faith

Stage 2: Mythic – Literal faith

Stage 3: Synthetic – Conventional faith

Stage 4: Individuative – Reflective faith

Stage 5: Conjunctive faith

Stage 6: Universalising faith

John Westerhoff's faith stages

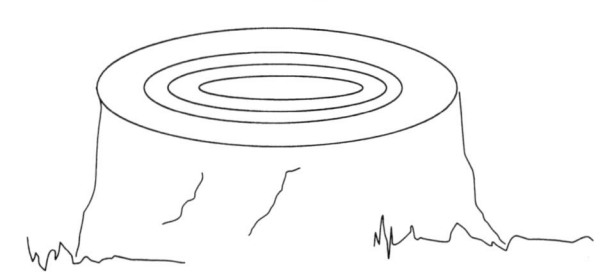

John Westerhoff saw faith as growing like the rings of a tree, each ring both adds to and changes the tree while building on what is already there. Originally he named four stages, and later changed this to three. The four original stages were Experienced faith (from early years, or a new faith system in adulthood), Affiliative faith (identification with the faith group in belief and practice), Searching faith (recognition of differences between group and personal belief challenge, to nudge us to question and decide where we stand), and Owned faith (where we have worked through the searching stage and personally own the faith). In his revised model, there are Affiliative, Searching and

Mature stages. (*Will Our Children Have Faith?* 1976 and *A Faithful Church,* 1981)

How do these match up with your own experience? (Make some notes to bring with you.)

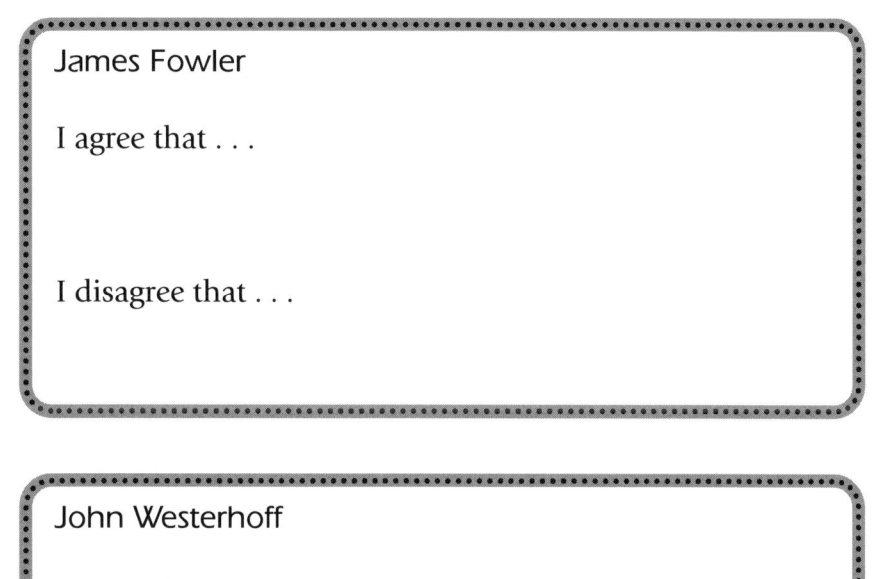

James Fowler

I agree that . . .

I disagree that . . .

John Westerhoff

I agree that . . .

I disagree that . . .

---

5. What you will need for session 3

Each person needs:
- their own copy of the course book
- a Bible
- notes on Fowler and Westerhoff

The group needs:
- large sheets of paper (flipchart pages or some lining paper)

- felt-tip pens/crayons
- pens/pencils

Optional extras:
- CD/tape player and music to play for worship

Checklist for session 3

☐ Preparation reading done

☐ Prayer support ongoing

☐ Course book and Bible

This week's Bible reading: John 20:24-29

But Thomas (who was called the Twin), one of the twelve, was not with them when Jesus came. So the other disciples told him, 'We have seen the Lord.' But he said to them, 'Unless I see the mark of the nails in his hands, and put my finger in the mark of the nails and my hand in his side, I will not believe.'

A week later his disciples were again in the house, and Thomas was with them. Although the doors were shut, Jesus came and stood among them and said, 'Peace be with you.' Then he said to Thomas, 'Put your finger here and see my hands. Reach out your hand and put it in my side. Do not doubt but believe.' Thomas answered him, 'My Lord and my God!' Jesus said to him, 'Have you believed because you have seen me? Blessed are those who have not seen and yet have come to believe.'

To think over . . .

In the end Thomas doesn't seem to need the proof he thought was essential, and Jesus doesn't seem to consider it necessary for us either. Why do you think this is? What's going on?

Do you sometimes feel like Thomas? Notice how Jesus addresses his misgivings and helps him through them. Jesus always meets us where we are.

Session 3
Growing together in faith

Learning outcomes

By the end of this session we will have
- prayed together and shared something of our faith journeys
- explored some models of faith development
- looked at how the whole church of people can grow in faith together

Introduction (10 minutes)

You will need some books of road maps.

Give each couple of people the destination and a starting place. They have to work out the best route to take. If you like you can put in some road works to avoid, or specify the time of travelling. Share the recommended routes. (Children could drive toy cars on a road mat.)

Prayer (5 minutes)

Play some quiet worship music on CD or tape to give everyone a chance to settle into God's company.

Now follow together the daily prayer outline on page 9, with this week's reading.

Practical organisation (5 minutes)

Sort out any practicalities or changes.

How does faith develop? (30 minutes)

1. A look at our own faith journeys

Reader

Obviously the details of your own faith journey are very personal, and you have no need to share them with anyone except God. But as you are working together, it will be helpful if you can talk over together the place you feel you are now in your faith, and share perhaps a 'broad brush stroke' outline of how you have arrived at this point today. As with the route in our first activity, all kinds of things have probably influenced the direction you have taken, and maybe some of the difficult times have actually helped you in your relationship with God, by a round-about route.

2. Models of faith development

Reader

Refresh your memories of the faith development models suggested by James Fowler and John Westerhoff, and use your notes to discuss them. See if you can come up with some other ways of drawing faith development. You might like to do this in pairs or threes, recording your faith development pictures on large sheets of paper to share with the whole group.

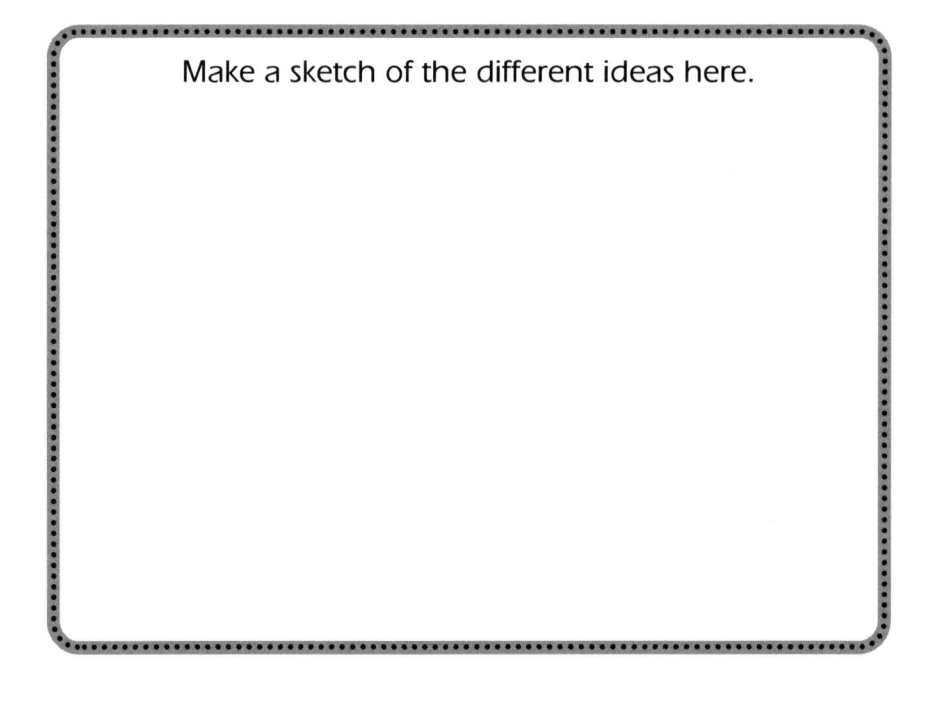

Make a sketch of the different ideas here.

How can we grow in faith together? (40 minutes)

Reader

Unless we are ourselves addressing our relationship with God, the children and young people we work with will lose out on good role models, and pick up a false idea of faith as a 'kids only' activity, to be discarded as part of being grown up. It really helps if everyone in the church is seen to be a lifelong 'student' or disciple, puzzling over deep truths and deep life questions, and grappling with an ever-enlarging understanding of God through the daily practicalities and challenges. As 'church members' we don't need to brush all our questions under the carpet and lock our brains away. Nor need we feel we ought to be experts. The people Jesus found he could best engage with were not necessarily the well-behaved, but the real and honest. All that is needed is to walk honestly with God, and that goes for the whole community – whatever the age.

> What would we like our children to learn about faith from the people in church who are adults?

> What would we like the adults in our church to learn about faith from the children and young people?

As you can see, we all help each other and learn from each other as we walk together in faith.

How do you think this might happen?

Look together at the following suggestions and add any other ideas which come up in your conversation.

- Decide to make daily prayer a way of life from now on.
- Reinstate the habit of 'saying Grace' before meals as a family.
- Use a faith nurture course with the children and young people which also includes nurture for the adults (such as *Living Stones* and *Bread and Wine People*).
- Use the planning sessions for your ministry as cell groups in which prayer and Bible study of relevant passages is an integral part.
- Have regular (annual or termly) times to go somewhere quiet and beautiful for prayer and refreshment.
- Encourage everyone of all ages to join a daily Bible reading or hearing scheme.
- Encourage a natural approach to prayer during your times with the children and young people, when all age groups take turns to lead others in praying.
- Have a library of suitable books to lend children and young people, and encourage parents to use the library as well.
- Have a regular (perhaps annual) church activity day designed for all ages to deepen their relationship with God and with one another and share in the celebration of their faith.
- Organise a church group to a Christian holiday programme such as Spring Harvest or Easter People or Taizé.

. . . and the other ideas

So that all our thinking today doesn't get lost, decide together on two or three definite plans to put in place straightaway. Write them down here, with a review date.

> My personal commitment . . .
>
> To be reviewed on..
>
> Our group commitment . . .
>
> To be reviewed on..

To finish

Read Luke 24:25-32.

This is the word of the Lord.
Thanks be to God
> **who draws alongside us wherever we are
> and walks with us, opening the scriptures to us,
> and making himself known
> in the breaking of bread.
> Amen.**

Group action

- Arrange for one person to display the faith development drawings somewhere in church and give a copy of the summary to the editor of the weekly news sheet.
- Remind each other of the date and place of the next session, and whose responsibility it will be to provide refreshments and so on.

Summary for the weekly news sheet

> **The DIY Co-op Training Course**
> At our third session we looked at how faith develops, and how we can nurture it in our church – both individually and collectively, as a lifelong journey for those of all ages. We've come up with some of our own models for faith development, and these are displayed at the back of church. How do they match up with your own experience? Session 4: 'Ways of telling the story' will be on (date) at (time), meeting at (address). Please keep us all in your prayers. Thank you.

Preparation reading for session 4

If anyone has a reading difficulty, please pair them up with a reading partner.

Heavenly Father,
 you already know and love
 each person in this community.
We ask that through our church
 the whole community may be blessed.
We pray especially for the babies, the toddlers,
 the children and the young people,
 and those who care for them.
May they all come to know
 how much you love them.
May they get to know you so well
 that the friendship lasts throughout their lives
 and on into heaven.
Amen.

1. Spiritual health check

At last week's session we spent quite a long time addressing our own walk with God. Take this opportunity to look again at the commitment you decided to make in your personal faith journey, and turn it into a reality during this week. Don't attempt something huge and unsustainable, but simple and realistic. A lot, abandoned, produces no growth and negative feedback to you. A very little, done faithfully, is valuable and works well.

2. Family stories

All families have their own special stories which are told and retold. It might be someone's terrible pregnancy, a flood or fire, a moment of acute embarrassment which still makes everyone helpless with laughter to remember, a dramatic pet story or a family claim to fame. There are stories we tell of a grandparent's childhood, so that the 'living memory' can stretch back nearly a hundred years. Telling the stories is all part of belonging to the family.

Increasingly we are learning to value stories again. There was a phase in which their authentic truths were often discounted in favour of the 'truth' of scientific data. Now, as we discover that science is not the precision answer we assumed it to be, and recognise that we all live in a cosmos of approximations and working hypotheses, we can once again relax about the human stories we love, and know them to be full of the deep truths we always suspected. Truth is a whole different dimension from fact.

Take, for instance, a love story like Romeo and Juliet. That is not detailed fact, but jammed full of the deep truth we all recognise about young love, conflict, tragedy and healing of a community through shared loss.

Last week we shared our own stories of faith with one another. During this week you may well have the privilege of hearing another's story of success, celebration, suffering or anger. The more we are ready to listen to one another's stories, the better we shall understand one another. So often we assume that we know where someone is coming from and react according to our interpretation. But suppose we are wrong? Suppose there is an unheard story which would make sense of behaviour which shocks or infuriates us? Suppose we sort out answers to questions people are not actually asking?

We need to cultivate the skill of attentive listening, both to one another, and to God. We need to model this listening for the children and young people in our care, and pass on the value of it to them, so that stories can be heard.

3. The God story

As Christians, the faith we share is like a family story. It is the story of love told through human and divine relationships, in the setting of the familiar, untidy and confusing world we are used to. The Bible is certainly no 'model answers' book of perfect people getting it right, is it? Nearly everyone gets it wrong, makes massive blunders, cheats and fails. That's one of the reasons we can trust its authentic ring – we read about real people behaving sometimes well and sometimes very badly.

Ours is a story of God's parenting; of creative and redeeming love, forgiveness and acceptance.

It is this story of God's love which has the power to set us free to live in full abundance so that we end up living the story ourselves. It's as if we are the pages still unwritten of the great story of love which needs to be told in and to every fresh generation. A story which is such liberating good news that we want everyone to hear it.

4. Telling the story with our lives

As we recognised in the last session, God's story is best told not in words but lives. That, after all, is the way God chose to do it, when Mary was approached by the angel Gabriel, and the Lord of earth and heaven was born as a human baby and laid in a feeding trough in the town of Bethlehem. We are called to be storytellers, and the way we tell the story will come freshly out of all the circumstances of our own lives. That, primarily, is how our children and young people will pick up the story.

Think back to your own childhood. You may remember very little of what you learnt, but you will probably have strong memories of particular people who influenced and affected your outlook and way of living. The children and young people in our care will pick up on the story we are really telling – the story we live – rather than the one we claim to be telling. And if the story we tell with words matches up with the one our lives tell, God's story will be told.

Think about the way this story of love is being told in your church. What happens to pass on the story of God's love week by week?

TEACHING THE TEACHERS

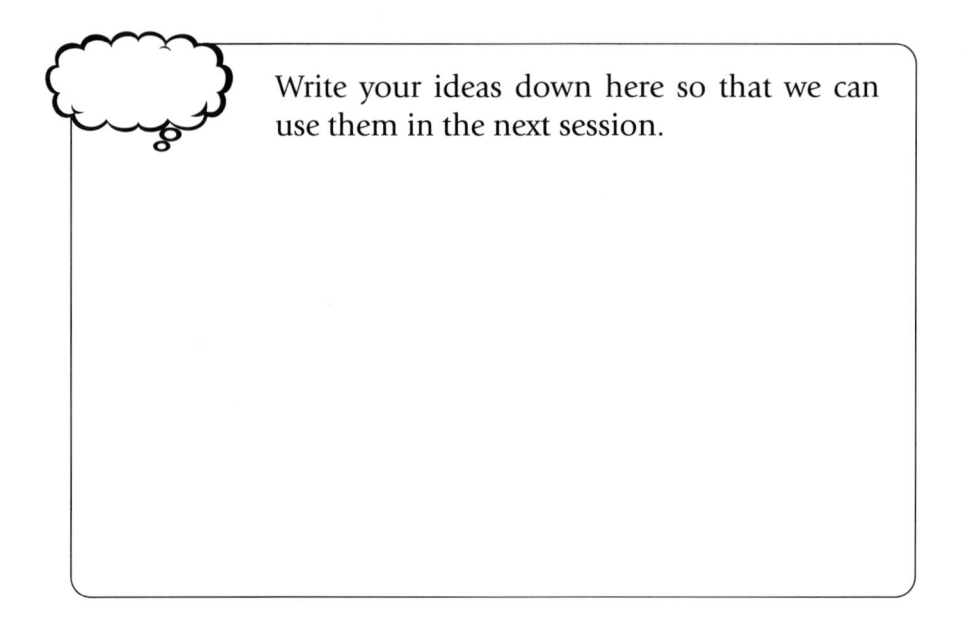

> Write your ideas down here so that we can use them in the next session.

5. What you will need for session 4

Each person needs:
- the course book with notes
- a Bible

The group needs:
- large sheets of paper (flipchart pages or some lining paper)
- felt-tip pens/crayons
- pens/pencils

Optional extras:
- CD/tape player and music to play for worship

Checklist for session 4

- [ ] Preparation reading done
- [ ] Prayer support continued
- [ ] Course book
- [ ] Bible

This week's Bible reading: Luke 6:37-49

'Do not judge, and you will not be judged; do not condemn, and you will not be condemned. Forgive, and you will be forgiven; give, and it will be given to you. A good measure, pressed down, shaken together, running over, will be put into your lap; for the measure you give will be the measure you get back.'

He also told them a parable: 'Can a blind person guide a blind person? Will not both fall into a pit? A disciple is not above the teacher, but everyone who is fully qualified will be like the teacher. Why do you see the speck in your neighbour's eye, but do not notice the log in your own eye? Or how can you say to your neighbour, "Friend, let me take out the speck in your eye," when you yourself do not see the log in your own eye? You hypocrite, first take the log out of your own eye, and then you will see clearly to take the speck out of your neighbour's eye.

'No good tree bears bad fruit, nor again does a bad tree bear good fruit; for each tree is known by its own fruit. Figs are not gathered from thorns, nor are grapes picked from a bramble bush. The good person out of the good treasure of the heart produces good, and the evil person out of evil treasure produces evil; for it is out of the abundance of the heart that the mouth speaks.

'Why do you call me "Lord, Lord," and do not do what I tell you? I will show you what someone is like who comes to me, hears my words, and acts on them. That one is like a man building a house, who dug deeply and laid the foundation on rock; when a flood arose, the river burst against that house but could not shake it, because it had been well built. But the one who hears and does not act is like a man who built a house on the ground without a foundation. When the river burst against it, immediately it fell, and great was the ruin of that house.'

To think over . . .

Hearing Jesus' words and seeing his life is compared to digging deeply and laying strong foundations for our own lives, so that the inevitable storms will not destroy us. Does this link up with your own experience? What implications are there for us in this ministry in which we find ourselves?

Session 4
Ways of telling the story

Learning outcomes

By the end of this session we will have
- prayed together
- seen storytelling in its widest context
- considered a range of creative storytelling methods

Introduction (10 minutes)

Tell one another about a person whose life has told you God's story.

Prayer (5 minutes)

Play some quiet worship music on CD or tape to give everyone a chance to settle into God's company.

Now follow together the daily prayer outline on page 9, with this week's reading.

Practical organisation (5 minutes)

Sort out any practicalities.

Ways of telling the story
(70 minutes including refreshments)

1. Being good stewards of God's story

> Have a look over the notes you made in the preparation for this session. Talk over with one another the ways in which you felt the church was passing on this story. Add other people's ideas here.

2. Nothing but the story

From your conversation, decide together on some general guidelines which mean that you are telling the story not just in 'story time' but in all your time together with the children and young people.

> The story, the story, the story

3. The art of storytelling
a) Reading as telling
Reader

Quite a lot of the library of books we know as the Bible records what for generations was spoken, rather than written. The oral tradition involves storytellers who learn a story and recount it faithfully, word perfect, so that it is handed down intact, mouth to ear to heart. For a time in this country the written word took over storytelling, and storytellers were a dying breed. I remember coming across a storyteller in a market place in Morocco, and felt I had travelled miles back through time. Yet now the storytelling business is thriving, and both children and adults can enjoy the collective experience of stories being woven.

Since we have a whole collection of such scripts in the Bible, it seems sensible to use such a rich resource, and something amazing seems to happen when we reconstitute those concentrates of writing with the living telling of them. Recently I read the story of Ruth at a preachers' conference, and several people, finding the words had suddenly come alive through the telling, assumed I was adding a lot of my own words. But I had added nothing at all. It was simply that the story was being related in its original medium.

So how do you do it?

- Read the story aloud several times as you prepare it.
- Aim to use the words as a script, so that you use not a 'reading voice' but a natural 'speaking voice'. Aim to make it sound like talking, not reading.
- Think about the meaning afresh every time you read it aloud, and imagine it. This is because thinking gaps are a natural part of talking. In reading we often ignore this. Gaps give the listener a chance to 'think the text', instead of being rushed artificially on to the next thought. Otherwise it's like giving people a whole glass of concentrated orange squash with no added water.
- Almost know the story off by heart so that you can tell it with eye contact.
- Keep your fingers moving down the page on either side of the columns of writing as you read. This way, whenever you look up you can immediately find your place again.

- Train your eye to look further ahead as you read. To practise this, look down at the words and then look up, seeing how much more of the sentence you can go on saying without looking. Try that now.
- If you like, try learning a Bible story off by heart, and then telling it, even without the script in front of you.

b) Using different versions of the story

We are blessed with a wide range of Bible translations and interpretive stories.

- Have a good browse around the local Christian bookshops and look at the same passage in its different forms before choosing ones appropriate for your particular group.
- As you read, use the checklist above to help you make a wise choice – not all lavishly illustrated versions are suitable. Check the text and style.
- Discard any well-meant gifts of outdated Bible story books, as our children and young people deserve better.

c) Illustrating the telling

Having visuals to accompany the telling is often helpful, especially if there are language difficulties in the group. Visuals also help concentration and focus, and can hint at the meaning. There are plenty of ways of doing the visuals . . .

- Use a story with illustrations. Gather the group around and show the pictures as you go, sometimes drawing attention to particular details in the picture, or asking questions to encourage their perception.
- Use a video clip of the story, or a series of slides.
- Display a few pictures related to the story as you tell it. These might be the landscape or the characters, and on paper or acetates. Add sound effects such as the sea or the wind.
- Draw as you go. Either the storyteller or an assistant sketches very simple illustrations, using a whiteboard, blackboard and coloured chalks, or OHP acetate and pens.
- The children doodle-draw as the story is told. Provide a roll of lining paper and crayons.
- Use a roll of paper already drawn on. It is unrolled like a scroll as the story is told.

- Display items of focus as the story is told (such as a lunch box for the feeding of the five thousand). Unpack these from a special box or bag, and pack them away again afterwards.

d) Acting out the telling

Children work through events in their lives by acting them out in play, so this is a very natural way for them to engage with the story on a number of levels. We're not talking about performance here, so perhaps we ought to say 'playing out' the story, rather than acting it.

- Spread out pieces of carpet or towels of landscape colours on the floor and move cut-out pictures or models around as the story is told. The children can have helped make some of the props before seeing them used in the telling.
- Use puppets. This might involve soft toys being held and talking the parts, a variety of cutlery and kitchen tools like spatulas and scrapers, faces drawn on fingers with cloth headdresses, paper bags with drawn faces and holes for finger arms, and real purpose-made puppets, both small and huge.
- A 'lion hunt' type of walk, where the groups sits or stands in a circle and there are actions which everyone joins in during the story.
- The storyteller tells the story in character, perhaps in a hint of costume.
- Two storytellers chat the story to each other, with the group earwigging.
- Everyone stands in a space and engages in the actions of the story (like hoisting the sails, casting and hauling in nets, sleeping, and pulling the boat up on the beach).
- Use a parachute (or very large sheet). Everyone stands around it and the sheet acts out the changing moods of the story with the gentle moving, violent flapping, or rise and fall of the fabric.
- Walk the whole group from area to area, giving stage directions as you go, so that everyone 'lives' the story.
- Have particular children taking parts and dressing up. The storyteller directs as the story progresses, quietly telling the children what to say and do, just before they say and do it.
- Write out particular words to be spoken in an appropriate

font and reading level on card shaped like speech bubbles. Give these to particular children to speak out during the story. Do the same thing with thoughts, but have these on thought bubble shapes of card.
- Use a complete script for a group of children or young people, ensuring that the font is clear and large enough for them to read easily. Have someone to check through with them any difficult words beforehand.

Group activity

Which methods might work well for your group with the following stories?

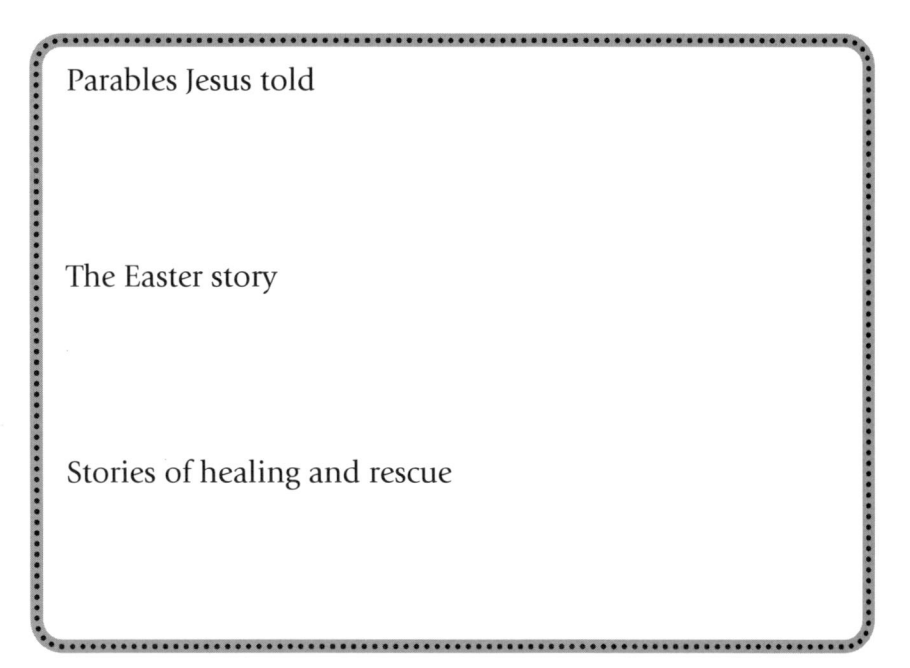

> Parables Jesus told
>
> The Easter story
>
> Stories of healing and rescue

Ring the changes; variety is the spice of life! Any good idea becomes dull if it's overused.

4. Responding to the story

Reader

Some resource materials give you specific help in enabling response. It is often helpful to have a short time of questions and comments where children and young people feel comfortable to raise any issues the story has opened up, and this is a time for the whole group to explore areas God is nudging us to look at.

All kinds of art and craft are valuable resource materials for response, and the finished product is not as important as the process. Even so, the rest of the congregation often find these tangible responses help their own understanding, by focusing on a particular truth, so sharing them with the whole congregation is very valuable.

Either prepare a particular set of materials and play music or chat the story through as you work (have an example completed to show them), or provide a number of possible materials and let the children choose how they want to express the story.

5. Your turn to have a go

In small groups, decide on a particular story and try preparing it for the others, using a method you haven't tried before. If you have children with you, experiment on them!

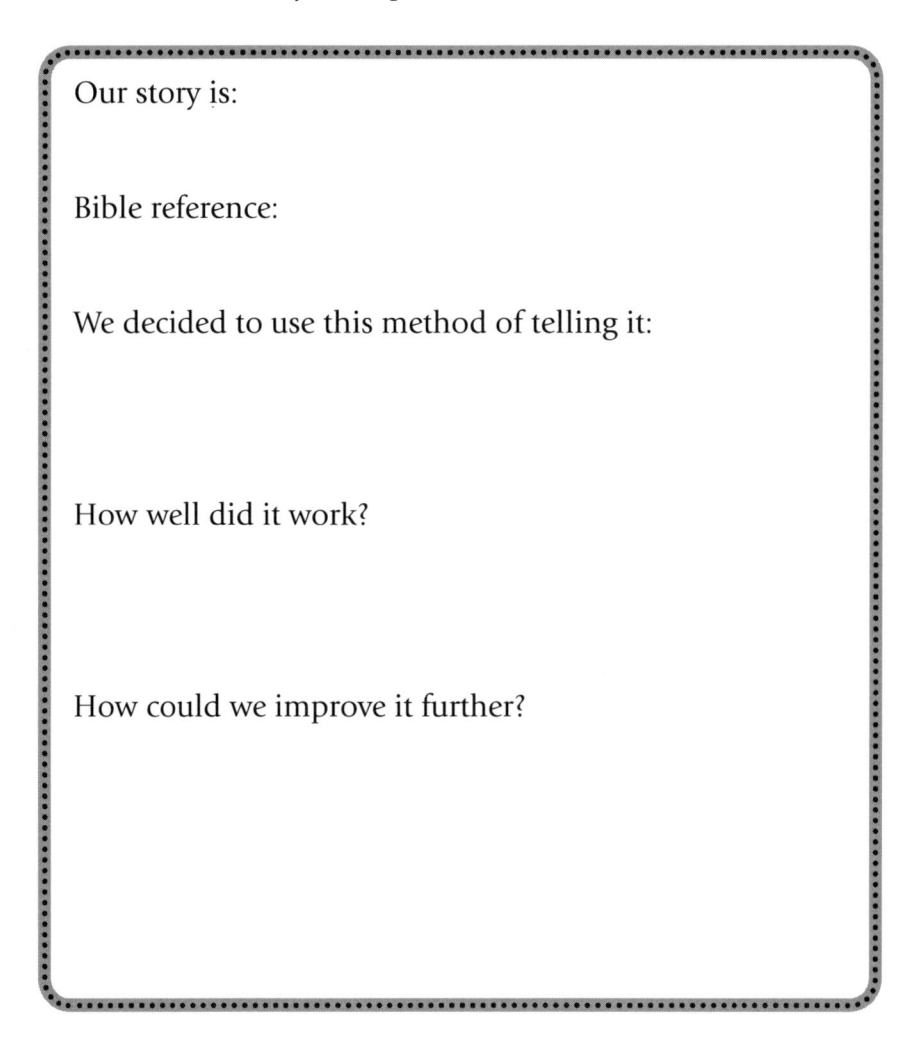

Our story is:

Bible reference:

We decided to use this method of telling it:

How well did it work?

How could we improve it further?

To finish

Read John 1:10-18

This is the word of the Lord.
Thanks be to God
  who tells us the story of love
  through the person of Jesus,
  who is alive, and continues to make the story known
  in lives set free to love as God loves.
Amen.

Group action

- Arrange a visit to the local Christian bookshop.
- Invest in the resources you need to tell the story.
- Remind each other of the date and place of the next session, and whose responsibility it will be to provide refreshments and so on.

Summary for the weekly news sheet

The DIY Co-op Training Course

At our fourth session we looked at different ways of telling the story of God's love, and tried some out. We will now be collecting resources for creative storytelling. Session 5: 'Behaviour management' will be on (date) at (time), meeting at (address). Please keep us all in your prayers. Thank you.

Preparation reading for session 5

If anyone has a reading difficulty, please pair them up with a reading partner.

Heavenly Father,
   you already know and love
   each person in this community.
We ask that through our church
   the whole community may be blessed.
We pray especially for the babies, the toddlers,
   the children and the young people,
   and those who care for them.
May they all come to know
   how much you love them.
May they get to know you so well
   that the friendship lasts throughout their lives
   and on into heaven.
Amen.

1. Suppose I can't cope

One of the things which worries people most about working with children and young people is the often secret fear that they won't be able to manage the challenging behaviour confidently. It is often this fear which is behind people offering to help but not lead. Often people feel embarrassed by this lack of confidence in behaviour management because they think of it as some kind of weakness in their personality. IT IS NOT!

Behaviour management is simply a skill which we can learn – like knitting or riding a bike. All we need is to know how to do it, and get some practice in. In the next session we will look at some of the basic skills and scripts, and we will put in a little practice as well.

2. Appropriate behaviour

Obviously different kinds of behaviour are acceptable and expected according to the situation. We behave differently relaxing at home from when we are at a task-driven committee meeting. What we are happy to see our children and young people up to when they are with a group of friends is not how we would expect them to behave in class. What is important is that the behaviour is appropriate, and that everyone agrees what *is* appropriate!

Some of the inappropriate behaviour we come across in church groups is actually a misunderstanding of what the expected and appropriate behaviour is. That's because church doesn't fit exactly with other situations they know. Is it relaxing with friends? Is it a formal situation like school? Is it club? Is it playground? Is it family gathering? Is it chat show? Is it lecture theatre? Is it performance and audience?

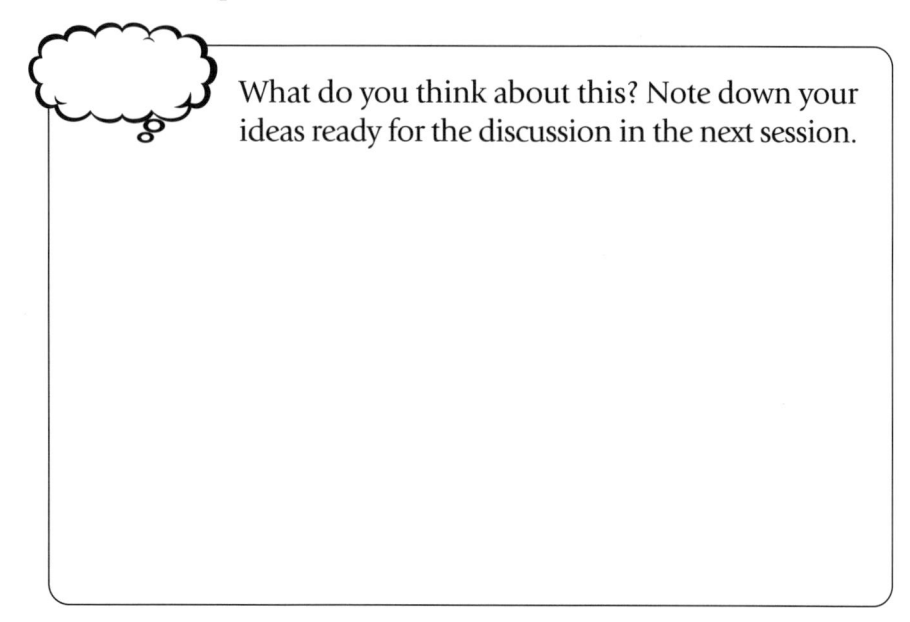

> What do you think about this? Note down your ideas ready for the discussion in the next session.

We all need to be taught how to behave appropriately, and we can't assume that children know already what is expected of them in this particular situation. When we are not sure about boundaries, we explore, like rabbits, until we hit against them.

3. The art of 'people watching'

Behaviour expectations do need to be realistic. The more we know and understand about the development of people – physical, mental, emotional and spiritual – the better equipped we will be in recognising what is realistic and what is not. We can also learn a great deal of wisdom from candid observation.

Get into the way of noticing the way babies, children and young people work. Notice the body language of their responses to different ways of being treated, for instance. Notice how they react to different tones of voice; notice what makes them settle and relax and what winds them up. Notice the effect on their behaviour of particular snacks, of blustery wind or hot sun, of the company they keep.

Dip into the education shelves in the library, watch some of the Open University programmes (you'll have to record them unless you don't sleep at night) and popular science series on television, and check out the nearest RE resource centre for books and videos you can borrow.

You can also learn from yourself. Think of situations in which you know you behave responsibly and well, and others where you instinctively find yourself wanting to misbehave. Work out for yourself what it is that switches on that 'disruptive' button and learn from it. I've noticed, for instance, that I get a strong desire to show people up and be disruptive if I suspect they are putting on airs and graces, or are pretending to know more than they do. Not a trait I like, but there it is. The boys I teach who have been excluded from school are exactly the same – just noisier and more physical in the way they go about it!

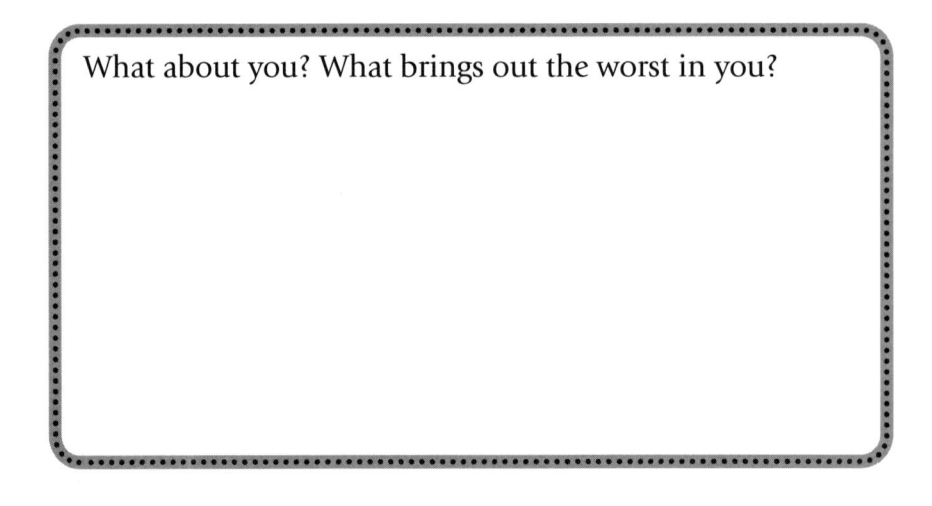

What about you? What brings out the worst in you?

4. Ways of managing behaviour

We will be referring to the following strategies during the next session. Read them through and note down any ideas or questions that occur to you.

a) Making the boundaries clear

When everyone is sitting in the circle, tell them how they are to behave so that everyone is safe and can enjoy the time of worship and learning together. As a group, work out perhaps two or three agreed rules and write these down clearly. Have them displayed at every session so you can refer people to them to remind them.

Not many will learn this at one sitting, so be prepared to teach it lots of times as necessary, without the 'how many more times . . .' sounding in your voice! If you think of it as teaching, and as any other ongoing task, like ironing, rather than 'telling off', you won't find it so stressful.

b) Model the behaviour you want to see

Children learn well from copying, and so the way you behave with them and each other will teach them far more than what you tell them to do. If they can see you listening attentively, being calm, being fair and encouraging fair practice, valuing and respecting, apologising for mistakes and humble enough to take criticism positively, then all this will influence the children's behaviour.

Sometimes we are not aware of the inconsistencies we model, so it's worth watching out for them. For instance, when we give constant attention to the disruptive children and let them do all the exciting things, hoping it will keep them quiet, what are the other children learning from our behaviour? When we state the consequences for disruptive or unkind behaviour and don't it carry out, what are we teaching the children?

If you want children to come and sit quietly in a circle, go across yourself and sit down quietly, asking them to join you there. Your modelled controlled and calm behaviour will be catching.

c) Using your voice effectively

You don't need a loud voice. In fact, if you shout a lot the children's noise level goes *up*. Quietly spoken teachers have quiet classrooms! But how you use your voice is important.

- When we are anxious, the pitch of our voice gets higher and we speed up, which gives away the fact that we're anxious! So consciously speak more slowly and in a low tone.
- Clear instructions are obeyed more readily, so don't drown your instructions in waffle. Be clear and concise, giving only one instruction at a time with younger children or those with learning difficulties.
- Your tone of voice tells whether you are irritated, angry, friendly or interested. Even young children can hear what you are really thinking when you admire their picture or tell them it's time to stop. So think before you speak!

d) Using your eyes effectively

Make eye contact with everyone in the group as you are speaking, because this says, 'I am including you personally.' If someone behaves inappropriately, looking at them until they resume attention reminds them of what they should be doing without interrupting the flow for the others. If you also stop speaking as you look, and then continue once they are attending again, there is no need for verbal reprimand. Don't refer to the behaviour at all. Your aim is not to make a point or an example but to have everyone attending.

Be sharp-eyed so that you notice the very start of problems. Make it clear that you have seen and know what is going on.

e) Catch them being good

We all thrive on a bit of encouragement, so it's good to encourage the children, noticing whenever they are trying hard in behaviour as in other things. We can help them grow in their Christian life by being encouragers.

A lot of inappropriate behaviour is attention-seeking. So if we respond by giving attention to the bad behaviour, the child has achieved the goal and learned that bad behaviour is the best way of getting the attention they crave. But we can turn this around by deliberately giving them attention when they are doing the right thing – often the times we ignore them. Catch them being good and praise them specifically, not generally, so they are being taught what good behaviour is, and what gets them your attention. ('Shane, that was very kind to lend Paul your crayon – well done'; 'Well done, Lizzy, you're sitting quiet and still ready for the story – very good listening!') What you *don't* do is remark sarcastically what a change it is from normal, or if they can sit like this now, why on earth aren't they doing it all the time.

f) Tactical ignoring

Rather than giving attention to people when they are behaving inappropriately for attention-seeking, ignore the attention-seeking behaviour while at the same time drawing attention to the behaviour of someone else close by who is behaving well, and give praise for that. The attention-seeker then often copies the behaviour that has been rewarded with attention. (For example, calmly continue to ask a question and choose someone to answer because you can see they are sitting quietly with their hand up, even if someone has already been shouting out the answer.)

g) Giving choices

We know ourselves that it is hard to lose face, and if we can give the children space to get out of a volcanic situation without losing face, it encourages them to act appropriately. If you give the child two (both appropriate) options to choose from, whichever they choose will bring about an acceptable solution.

For instance: 'Jamie, you're finding it hard to behave sensibly next to Ross this morning. You can choose either to behave properly next to your friend or to sit and behave properly next to me.'

Or: 'Bradley, we're all clearing up now. You can choose what job to do – either to help Mike with the chairs or Mandy with the pencils.'

Or: 'You need to put your cards away now, Emily. You can put them either in your bag or in the treasure box on the table.'

5. What you will need for session 5

Each person needs:
- the course book with notes
- a Bible

The group needs:
- large sheets of paper (flipchart pages or some lining paper)

- felt-tip pens/crayons
- pens/pencils

Optional extras:
- CD/tape player and music to play for worship

Checklist for session 5

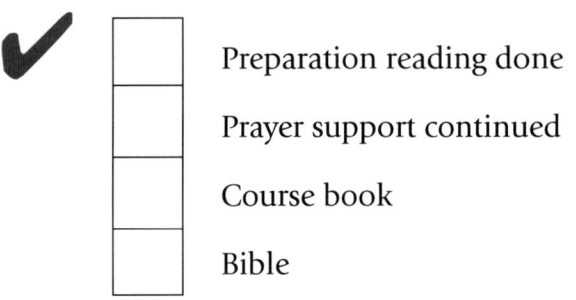

- [ ] Preparation reading done
- [ ] Prayer support continued
- [ ] Course book
- [ ] Bible

This week's Bible reading: Psalm 145:8-9, 13b-14, 17-18

The Lord is gracious and merciful,
slow to anger and abounding in steadfast love.
The Lord is good to all,
and his compassion is over all that he has made . . .
The Lord is faithful in all his words,
and gracious in all his deeds.
The Lord upholds all who are falling,
and raises up all who are bowed down . . .
The Lord is just in all his ways,
and kind in all his doings.
The Lord is near to all who call on him,
to all who call on him in truth.

To think over . . .

Perhaps above all else we just need to take these qualities of our God to heart and try to copy them in the way we live.

Session 5
Behaviour management

Learning outcomes

By the end of this session we will have
- prayed together
- agreed on what we consider appropriate behaviour for the children and young people in our church
- discussed ways of avoiding problems in behaviour
- discussed ways of defusing problems when they do happen
- tried out some of the strategies to practise them

Introduction (5 minutes)

Share with each other the situations which make you want to behave badly (or which used to, if you've grown out of it!).

Prayer (5 minutes)

Play some quiet worship music on CD or tape to give everyone a chance to settle into God's company.
Now follow together the daily prayer outline on page 9.

Practical organisation (5 minutes)

Sort out any practicalities.

Behaviour management
(75 minutes including refreshments)

There was quite a lot of reading to get through during the week. Spend a few minutes looking through the material to refresh your memories.

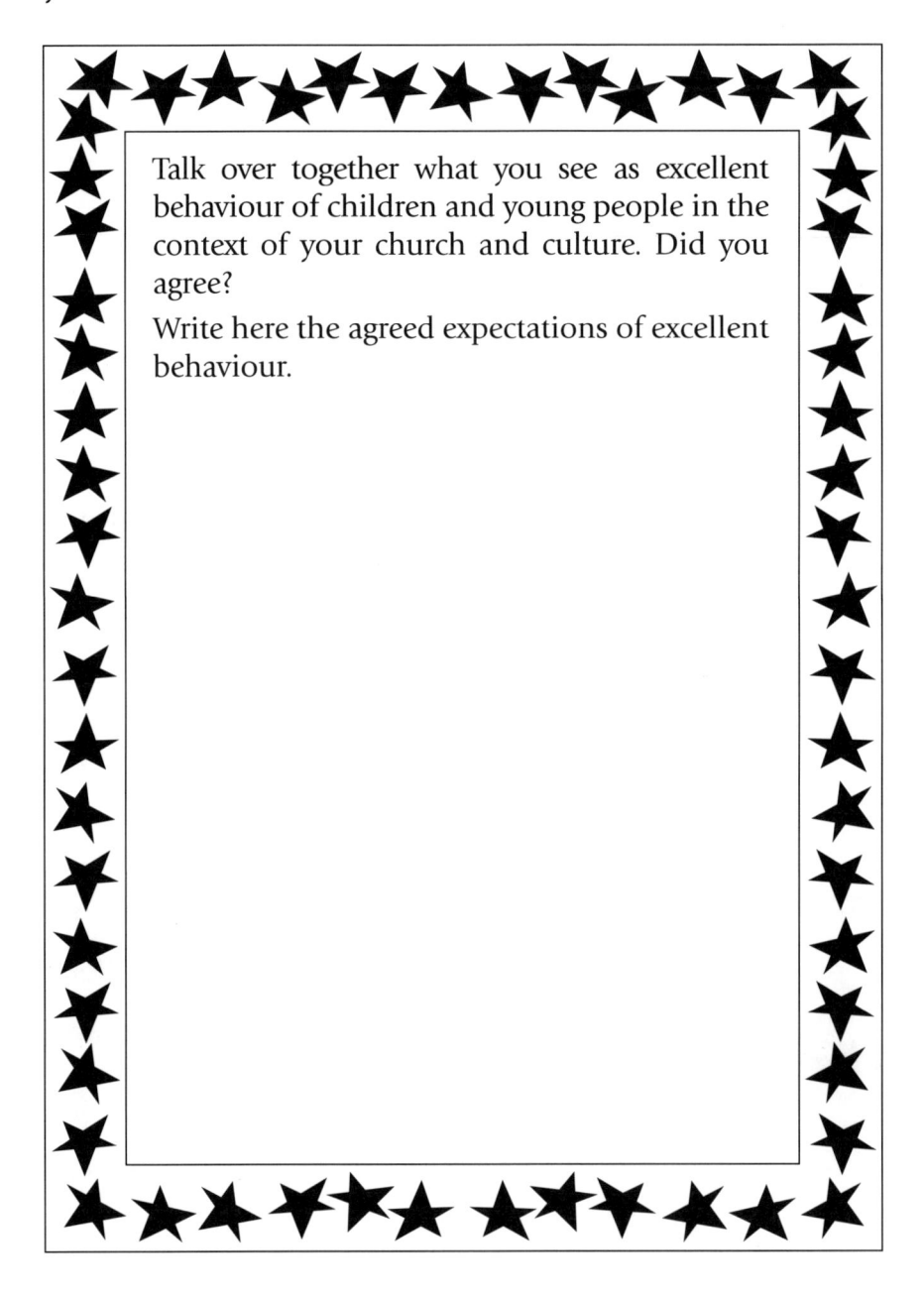

> Talk over together what you see as excellent behaviour of children and young people in the context of your church and culture. Did you agree?
>
> Write here the agreed expectations of excellent behaviour.

1. Getting off to a good start

Reader

Prevention is better than cure, and in behaviour management that means setting things up so that there are fewer opportunities for inappropriate behaviour to start, and more opportunities for appropriate behaviour to develop and become a habit. Have a look at these guidelines and once again relate them to how they can be put into practice in your own situation:

- **Be prepared and organised beforehand**. That way you can focus on the children and young people from the moment they come in, greeting them by name and listening to their news in a relaxed atmosphere. Having things prepared also gives the children and young people the signal that this is a place where things are done in an orderly way, and the implication is that orderly, responsible behaviour is the expectation.
- **Know the children's names**. Being known by your name reinforces the sense of belonging, of feeling safe and confident.
- **Have the room set out ready**. Have chairs grouped in the circle, or a sitting place marked clearly in some way – perhaps a large rug. Have worktables already put together with the art/craft equipment there. Have some praise and worship music already playing so that the children hear it as they get near. Encourage parents to help their young children take off outdoor clothes and bring their child to one of the helpers, rather than leaving them at the door.
- **Make sure all the adults understand that their job is to interact with the children, not with each other in a holy huddle.** (Sometimes this happens because helpers aren't sure how to talk to the children, so let newcomers shadow 'old-handers' to give them confidence.)
- **Have an open-ended starter activity.** This means that early arrivals can begin straightaway, once they have been welcomed.
- **Look out for the timid and tearful ones.** The time of arrival is often crucial in calming fears. Older children (particularly older children with behaviour difficulties, I've found!) are specially good at befriending little ones and making them welcome.
- **Have the ground rules displayed.** If they are illustrated even the younger children can read them.

2. General strategies

Reader

Now work your way together through each of the strategies described in the preparation reading, relating the situations to ones you experience in your ministry with children and young people, and seeing how they might be applied. Practise saying the 'scripts' to each other. Practise giving clear instructions. Use the time as a workshop so that the strategies 'take root' in your thinking and outlook. Involve the children as you work.

> Make a note of any useful ideas which come up in your conversation.

3. Specific needs

Reader

If you have a child with particular behaviour problems, still look at which of the general strategies help in managing the behaviour. The underlying order and fairness is valuable whatever is causing the difficulty. But if the behaviour is part of a behaviour disorder syndrome (such as ADHD or autism, Down's or Tourette's) you will need extra support in place for this particular person. Either have the parent accompanying the child, or ask for a volunteer from the congregation to take on this role of care and support for a child with specialised needs. They will need to talk quietly to the child throughout the session, keeping them focused, dealing with their burning questions straightaway, perhaps holding and comforting them, playing the games and taking part in the activities as a couple, and taking them out for a breather if necessary. It all depends on the precise needs of the child. The fact that such carers are provided speaks of God's love and acceptance of each one of us, with all our individual specialised needs.

> In all your thinking
> keep in mind the Bible reading for the week
> from Psalm 145.

4. Defusing battles

Reader

The truth is that however carefully you arrange the room, learn your scripts and manage the group behaviour, there may well be still those nightmare times when battles erupt and you wonder why on earth you are involved in this work!

Some hopefully helpful hints . . .

- Talk and pray it over with someone you trust, who won't overreact.
- Don't assume it's all your fault and you're useless because it happened.
- Don't assume it would be far better if certain people were banned.
- Bear in mind there may be all kinds of reasons for this conflict which are not related to you or this session. Be sensitive to this.
- Learn from the experience by looking at what triggered it.
- Recognise the signs of a potential conflict and intervene sooner rather than later, by changing the activity, splitting the warriors on some valid pretext unrelated to their spleen, and not taking sides or treating it as a big issue.
- Don't enter the battle yourself. Children and young people overwhelmed with emotions in themselves need adults who can hold that anger for them safely, and it is sometimes our privilege to do just that.

- It isn't necessarily the crying child who is the victim and the fuming one who is the cruel tyrant. And anyway, at the moment, both need help in calming down.
- Humour is very good at easing tensions. Relax your face muscles, breathe deeply and smile. But always use humour to help, never as a weapon.
- *Love them, enjoy them, learn from them, pray for them!*

To finish

Read 1 Corinthians 13:1-13

This is the word of the Lord.

Thanks be to God
   who is love in all its fullness,
   who loves us completely
   and loves all those with whom we work.
Amen.

Group action

- Arrange for one person to give a copy of the summary to the editor of the weekly news sheet and to have copies of the reading preparation for session 6 available at the back of the church.
- Remind each other of the date and place of the next session, and whose responsibility it will be to provide refreshments and so on.

Summary for the weekly news sheet

> ### The DIY Co-op Training Course
> At our fifth session we looked at behaviour management, and how we can create a church environment which encourages and values thoughtful, responsible behaviour. Session 6: 'When we're all together' will be on (date) at (time), meeting at (address). As this relates to the whole church in a particular way, you are all welcome to join us for this final session of the course. Copies of the reading preparation for this are available at the back of the church. Please keep us all in your prayers. Thank you.

Preparation reading for session 6

If anyone has a reading difficulty, please pair them up with a reading partner.

Heavenly Father,
 you already know and love
 each person in this community.
We ask that through our church
 the whole community may be blessed.
We pray especially for the babies, the toddlers,
 the children and the young people,
 and those who care for them.
May they all come to know
 how much you love them.
May they get to know you so well
 that the friendship lasts throughout their lives
 and on into heaven.
Amen.

1. Learning to be a community of love

We get so used to the word 'church' meaning the special building that we tend to forget that the building only came to be known as 'a church' because it was the place where 'the church' gathered week by week. 'The church' is us – the gathered people of God.

What does it mean, then, to be 'the church'? Another word we have become used to hearing is 'member'. We talk about being church members, and that gives us a clue, because 'members' are body parts. It follows that if we are church 'members' we are bits of a body. What kind of body? We are talking about the Body of Christ (or Messiah, or God's Anointed One).

Now this is where it all gets rather challenging. We know from the gospels how Jesus lived. It was a life which expressed the love of God in human terminology.

From the accounts of eye witnesses and collective memory, we see Love engaging with real people at their times of deep need and healing, eating and drinking with the socially despised and marginalised, the well-heeled, the religious, the blatant sinners and the social climbers. We see encounters with the elderly, the middle-aged, the young people, the children and the babies, the dying, the celebrating, the hated occupying military and the mentally disturbed. We see teaching in riddles and stories, often with no explanations offered, a lightweight attitude to possessions and rights, and an uncompromising insistence on forgiveness, truth, mercy and justice.

If, as church, we are body parts of such a Body, we might expect the church to be recognised by a similar lifestyle. Think it over. Where in the church do you recognise the life of Christ, and where is there a contrast?

2. Wearing our L-plates

It's probably clear from your thinking that we're certainly not experts or perfect in being the church, but we are aware of being learners, students or disciples. And perhaps that's the most important thing to acknowledge. Learner drivers are not banished from the roads – they'd never learn if they were – but we make it a point of law that they display their L-plates. I think we need to remember our L-plates, to remind ourselves that we are lifelong disciples, in an ongoing process of learning how to live as the loving community we are called to be.

3. Household of faith

Such a process is not going to be without its tensions and conflicts, but these are actually the creative places of deep learning, if we care to use them as such. How are we going to learn to forgive, for instance, unless we get in some practice in real situations? How are we going to learn about loving respect for those we disagree with if we insist on fragmenting our household into the groups of those who agree with us? How are we to learn from one another's culture, age group and personality if we never engage with one another or worship together?

The image of a household is quite a helpful one. Thinking of it in its broadest sense, it includes all who visit, work or live there permanently. A household might include those of all different age groups, married and single, impoverished and comfortably off. The church is rather like a household of faith.

4. Getting together

As church – as this community of love – we need times when we all get together. Perhaps you have a time after worship when people can gather for refreshments. Such times are of immense value, and really ought to be thought of as part of the worship, because they are such an important part of this calling we have. Perhaps we should have this time during the service rather than after it, as an extension of the exchange of Peace, or of Communion. (But don't worry, that's not essential!)

There are other ways we can work at building community and breaking down some of the barriers that have grown up over the years. Churches enjoy meals together from time to time, parties, barn dances, fairs and so on. At Easter the different churches often gather together, organising a shared walk and reflection on Good Friday. Church groups go on holiday together, either on their own or with another church, or at one of the larger venues like Spring Harvest, Walsingham or World Village.

5. Worshipping together

It is also important that at least on some occasions in the year we worship together, but that raises all kinds of difficulties, as you have probably experienced. There's the problem of noise, with babies and toddlers making it difficult for the other people to concentrate on what they're doing. There's the problem of some people feeling left out, and, according to what style the worship takes, this might be either the young or the adults. There's the danger of turning whole church worship into children's worship with adults present, or adult worship with children present. There's the difficulty of length of service, appropriate hymns, an unrealistic amount of preparation needed and the inflexible design of the building.

So is it worth it? Or is it better to agree that while it's a good ideal, it isn't a practical possibility.

If we take seriously our calling to be a community of love with our L-plates displayed, I don't think we can just opt out, however tempting it might be. But what we can do is rethink what it might mean to come together in worship, and use the challenges as God-given opportunities for learning the love community skills of communication, mutual respect and acceptance, sharing, sacrificial giving, humility, thoughtfulness and kindness, forgiveness and patience. In fact, the list is very similar to the list of the fruits of the Spirit in Galatians (5:22-25), isn't it? 'Love, joy, peace, patience, kindness, generosity, faithfulness, gentleness and self-control.' In the next sentence Paul goes on to say, 'If we live by the Spirit let us also be guided by the Spirit.'

6. Going against the flow

Joining together is counter-cultural. It feels specially hard for us because it is in complete contrast to the current norm of splitting the natural community into peer groups and interest groups. Instead, it celebrates the value of being together, and proclaims that all the different age groups need each other in order to grow into a healthy, trusting community. In standing up for this, against the dislocated, suspicious and fragmented culture we inhabit, the church is being salt and light.

7. What you will need for session 6

Each person needs:
- the course book with notes
- a Bible

PREPARATION READING FOR SESSION 6

The group needs:
- large sheets of paper (flipchart pages or some lining paper)
- small squares of paper for everyone
- felt-tip pens/crayons
- pens/pencils
- glue sticks

Optional extras:
- CD/tape player and music to play for worship

Checklist for session 6

☐ Preparation reading done

☐ Prayer support continued

☐ Course book

☐ Bible

This week's Bible reading: Psalm 148:7-14

Praise the Lord from the earth,
    you sea monsters and all deeps,
    fire and hail, snow and frost,
    stormy wind fulfilling his command!
Mountains and all hills, fruit trees and all cedars!
Wild animals and all cattle, creeping things and flying birds!
Kings of the earth and all peoples,
    princes and all rulers of the earth!
Young men and women alike, old and young together!
Let them praise the name of the Lord,
    for his name alone is exalted;
    his glory is above earth and heaven.
He has raised up a horn for his people,
    praise for all his faithful,
    for the people of Israel who are close to him.
Praise the Lord!

To think over . . .

Imagine for a minute what this vision would be like. Share the dream. Share the longing for the kingdom and then say the Lord's prayer, slowly and reflectively.

Session 6
When we're all together

Learning outcomes

By the end of this session we will have
- prayed together
- considered what are the benefits of getting together for worship
- looked at how the challenges can become opportunities
- explored some practical suggestions

Introduction (10 minutes)

Give everyone (including the children) a small square of paper and have the pens and pencils available. On your piece of paper draw someone else in the church community and stick all the pictures on a large sheet cut out in the shape of a church. You can draw several people if there's time. Make sure that all age groups in the church are represented. Lay the finished picture down in the centre of the group as a focus during the time of prayer.

Prayer (5 minutes)

Play some quiet worship music on CD or tape to give everyone a chance to settle into God's company.

Now follow together the daily prayer outline on page 9.

Practical organisation (5 minutes)

Sort out any practicalities.

What does it mean to be church?
(70 minutes including refreshments)

Using the reading and your notes and ideas, talk over in small groups what it means to be church, and how this matches up with the reality.

> Record the main ideas on the large sheets, and as you share insights, note them down in your book.

Reader

When we work from this end, rather than the 'all-age worship' end, we can see that getting together in worship is far more of a different attitude or outlook than a particular style or format. It is being sensitive to the needs of all those in the church community – all the age groups and cultures represented. It's an attempt to experience the word and sacrament together in ways that all can access, so that none is excluded. In such a climate, the community skills of real loving have to be practised. Underlying such skills is God's love present in the members of his Body as we travel in faith together. We all need humility to recognise our need of others on this faith journey.

SESSION 6: WHEN WE'RE ALL TOGETHER

What gifts do the different age groups bring to the whole community? (Don't look at my ideas until you've come up with your own – you'll probably have thought of plenty that I haven't.)

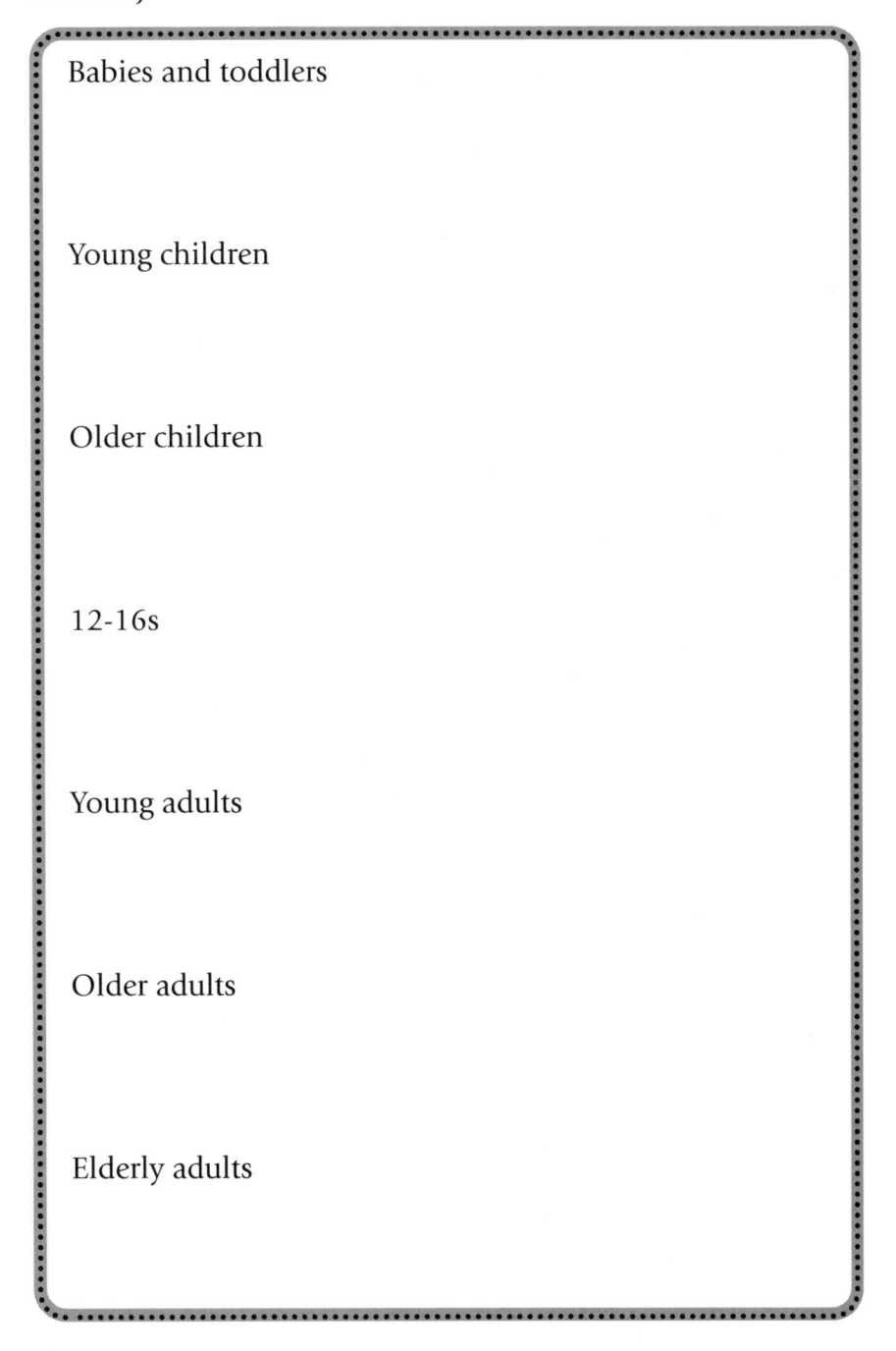

> Babies and toddlers
>
> Young children
>
> Older children
>
> 12-16s
>
> Young adults
>
> Older adults
>
> Elderly adults

Now you can look at my ideas if you like!

Babies and toddlers are experts at teaching us so much about our human vulnerability and basic needs, the miracle of life, the natural goodness and openness of being a new human, and the focus on 'now'.

Young children are experts in teaching us all about wonder and curiosity, the value of questions, and the honesty of being yourself and saying what you think!

Older children are experts at teaching us experiment and wholehearted living, energy and enthusiasm, deep thinking about the unknown and unseen, and fairness and justice down to the last crisp.

12-16s are experts both at refusing to have any truck with hypocrisy and at using technology in worship. They help us balance idealism with reality, have a zeal and passion when they get praying and will not let the church become complacent. They have a sharpness of wit which can challenge flabby attitudes or areas of blindness, and they dream dreams. (So *that's* why they take so long getting up!)

Young adults hold the needs and ways of the world in balance with the worship of the church. They encourage the church to relate to the wider world, and are impatient with outdated systems which have become destructively entrenched. Some are beginning to raise families, and need the community's love and support in these relationships.

Older adults hold the church to valuing both the traditional and the fresh. They work at taking decisions responsibly. They have great experience and skill in many areas through life and work.

The very elderly have the wisdom and experience of many years of living, and a lifetime of prayer. They are often gifted at seeing what the really important issues are, since they are aware of death.

So how do we plan for the whole community worshipping together? Here are some general principles to think and talk about:

- Involve age group representatives in the planning.

- Use all the senses alongside language (such as projected pictures of people and landscapes, natural sounds and music, lighting and fragrance, stones to touch).

- Think of what you all have in common (all the human things, like being hungry/thirsty and satisfied; knowing sadness and happiness; feeling lonely/left out and accepted; looking forward to something; wondering why; having favourite colours) and use these areas as examples rather than just the written word and abstract concepts.

- Don't feel you've all got to be doing the same thing at the same time. While the adults are praying for the church and the world in their way, gather the very young children to a special prayer carpet with a leader, who quietly prays with the children using pictures or symbols, and have the older children taken on a prayer walk around the building or praying in small groups with their leaders.

- Sometimes give words a rest altogether. Have images and music and invite people to pray (in a time of confession or intercession, or praise and thanksgiving) in their hearts. Invite everyone to move around the building while recorded music is playing, and pray using the beauty of the building itself to inspire them.

- Introduce a talk or reflection on a reading with a short sketch, a mime or clip from a radio programme or film track, or a short interview.

- Have different people reading the characters' parts in a Bible reading, or acting them out. Have some sections which everyone can join in.

- Involve all age groups in the various 'jobs' during worship.

- Have streamers and worship flags available for people to use during the hymns – not as a performance but as their worship.

- Have a selection of percussion instruments for playing during some of the hymns, as appropriate.

- Make sure everyone can see and hear what's going on.

Above all, enjoy being the community of God's people, brothers and sisters together.

> **In small groups . . .**
>
> Using the readings or theme for the next planned service, give each small group a section of the worship to plan, using the guidelines above. Then share your ideas and write down the suggestions.

To finish

Read Psalm 133

This is the word of the Lord.
Thanks be to God
    who gives us the grace
    to live together
    in love and unity.
Amen.

Group action

- Arrange for one person to give a copy of the summary to the editor of the weekly news sheet.
- Have a party! You deserve it – well done!

Summary for the weekly news sheet

> **The DIY Co-op Training Course**
>
> At our final session we looked at worshipping together, and how we can plan to include everyone in our church community. Thank you all for your prayer support during the course. Please continue to pray for our children and young people and their families.

Review and refresh

You will find it helpful to review your ministry regularly, at least annually. What follows are some suggested areas of discussion at such reviews, and a suggested format for a quiet day together, for your spiritual refreshment, both as individuals and as Body members!

First, the reviews . . .

Begin with a short time of worship.

With both thanksgiving and awareness of need, pray for the church, the children, young people and their families. Pray for each other.

Read through your policy document, making notes of any changes, and raising any areas of concern.

- What has worked well?
- What needs to be adjusted?
- What areas are still not being addressed?
- What have we learnt?

Look back at your faith journeys (page 41).

- Where do you feel you are now?
- How is the daily prayer and Bible reading going?
- How about the developing faith of the children and young people – are they growing?

What can happen at review meetings is that lots of good ideas are spoken and then lost because no one is given the specific task of implementing them. To make sure you catch and hold the good ideas, write them down as the meeting goes on (you could appoint a 'minutes taker' for this) and check that any actions to be taken are also written down, with the name of whoever is willing to do them. As ever, make sure the workload is spread.

Decide who will write the reviewed policy and have copies given to everyone concerned.

To finish . . .

Read Ephesians 6:13-18, 23-24

Therefore take up the whole armour of God, so that you may be able to withstand on that evil day, and having done everything, to stand firm. Stand therefore, and fasten the belt of truth around your waist, and put on the breastplate of righteousness. As shoes for your feet put on whatever will make you ready to proclaim the gospel of peace. With all of these, take the shield of faith, with which you will be able to quench all the flaming arrows of the evil one. Take the helmet of salvation, and the sword of the Spirit, which is the word of God.

Pray in the Spirit at all times in every prayer and supplication. To that end keep alert and always persevere in supplication for all the saints.

Peace be to the whole community, and love with faith, from God the Father and the Lord Jesus Christ. Grace be with all who have an undying love for our Lord Jesus Christ.

This is the word of the Lord
Thanks be to God.

And now a suggested approach to a quiet, spiritual refreshment day . . .

Where?
It's a good idea to go somewhere different. Look at the possibility of a retreat house, convent, friary or priory (contact your Diocesan Office, or equivalent, for information). You might be able to borrow someone's caravan for the day, or a room and garden of a friend's home.

How long?
Long enough to have a good sense of space, and short enough to be practical, given our other responsibilities. A day might begin at about 10.30am and end by 3.30pm.

What?
Include a short time of worship, suggested Bible passages and books to read, and a variety of art/craft materials to use. A bring-and-share lunch cuts down on organisation and workload, but still speaks about a community of shared love. Have some times of fasting from words, times of quiet background music perhaps, and a time of sharing and fellowship over a cup of tea at the end. Finish with prayer.

Suggestions for Bible passages
- The whole of Mark's Gospel, read straight through.
- The book of Ruth, read straight through.
- The book of Jonah, read straight through.
- Psalm 139:1-18
- Psalm 23
- Acts 10, and 11:1-18
- Acts 27 and 28
- John 9
- John 4

Appendix: Useful resources

Basic resources people have found helpful	**Possible sources**
Paper – white, coloured, shiny, crêpe, tissue, various sizes	*Printers, packing firms, congregation, recycled weekly handouts, wrapping paper, lining paper, wallpaper*
Card – thick, thin, large, small	*Factories, shops, printers, recycled greetings cards and packaging*
Boxes	*Shoe shops, contact lens users, congregation, recycled cream cheese packs, food cartons*
Pens, pencils, crayons, sharpeners, scissors, craft knife, paints, paint trays, brushes, sponges, roller and tray, gluesticks, washable PVA glue, sellotape, wire, wire cutters	*Worth paying for good quality, both safe and effective. Voting booth extras (good for sharpeners and pencils). Also try old baking trays, foil dishes*
Plastic protective sheeting, overalls, washing-up bowl, jug and towel	*DIY/camping shops. Refuse sacks. Old shirts*
Cotton wool, pipe cleaners, paper fasteners, self-adhesive coloured labels, balls of wool and string, rubber bands, foil, greaseproof paper, nails, wood offcuts, candles	*Congregation, bargain shops*

Basic resources people have found helpful	Possible sources
Pictures, clipart, acetates, posters	*Calendars, magazines, newspapers, travel brochures, shops, Internet*
Printed resources – course books, work books, children's reference Bible, Bible atlas, Bibles, Bible story books, books of prayer, picture books of the Holy Land, world map, globe	*Borrow from libraries and diocesan resource centres, share with other churches in your neighbourhood, buy from Christian bookshops and publishers, gifts from congregation, Bible Society*
Carpet tiles/story carpet, church toys, dressing-up clothes, length of blue cloth, puppets	*Friendly carpet shops, willing helpers in congregation, local WI, offcuts, leftovers*
Access to CD and tape player, parachute, OHP and screen or white wall, flipchart, blackboard and coloured chalks, musical instruments	*Parish resources, loan from congregation, share with local schools/churches*